Praise for
Unfinished

Packed with relatable stories and helpful exercises, *Unfinished* encourages and guides us to understand and accept who we really are. If you want to be your best, most authentic, this book is for you.

—Phil Gerbyshak
Author, Sales Expert, and Recovering Self-Doubter

Chris Schindler is an authentic, talented leader and has written a book that is practical and applicable. Discovering one's strengths, being authentically courageous, and seeking to learn helps leaders forge enduring relationships, even during times of constant evolution. This book offers a practical perspective for self-development and growth!

—Melanie (Mel) Sullivan
Ed.D., MBA, Chief People Officer

Unfinished is a book that will keep you captivated until the end, as it is filled with authentic stories and tips to help you meet your true self in the present moment with grace and acceptance of life's perfect unfoldment.

—Susan K. Wehrley
Life & Business Coach, *BIZremedies.com*

Where do I even start? I was drawn into *Unfinished* before I finished page one. Author Chris Schindler has created a wonderful opportunity for us to both embrace the beauty—and acceptance—of an *Unfinished* life and to delve into the experience of our own growth journey. Packed full of moments for reflection, one of my favorite *Try It* activities in her book involved identifying people in our lives as depleting our energy or boosting our energy. This simple activity has given me insight into who I will be intentional about spending time with, as well as committing to how I want to show up for others. Schedule your retreat time and sneak away with Chris's book! Your life will be better for it.

—Aleta Norris
Author of *Women Who Spark* & *Women Who Spark After 50;*
Co-founder of Living As A Leader

UNFINISHED

UNLOCK YOUR SUPERPOWERS, LIVE WITH PURPOSE, AND DISCOVER LIMITLESS POSSIBILITIES

UNFINISHED

UNLOCK YOUR SUPERPOWERS, LIVE WITH PURPOSE, AND DISCOVER LIMITLESS POSSIBILITIES

CHRISTINE LUKOVICH SCHINDLER

AUTHOR ACADEMY elite

Unfinished © 2023 by Christine Lukovich Schindler. All rights reserved.

Published by Author Academy Elite
PO Box 43, Powell, OH 43065
www.AuthorAcademyElite.com

All rights reserved. This book contains material protected under international and federal copyright laws and treaties. Any unauthorized reprint or use of this material is prohibited. No part of this book may be reproduced or transmitted in any form or by any means, electronic or mechanical, including photocopying, recording, or by any information storage and retrieval system, without express written permission from the author.

Identifiers:
LCCN: 2022922329
ISBN: 979-8-88583-165-9 (paperback)
ISBN: 979-8-88583-166-6 (hardback)
ISBN: 979-8-88583-167-3 (ebook)

Available in paperback, hardback, e-book, and audiobook

Any Internet addresses (websites, blogs, etc.) and telephone numbers printed in this book are offered as a resource. They are not intended in any way to be or imply an endorsement by Author Academy Elite, nor does Author Academy Elite vouch for the content of these sites and numbers for the life of this book.

To Sam
My daughter and my inspiration.

Acknowledgments

Self-doubt has accompanied me throughout my life, perfectly synced with people who encouraged me during pivotal moments. I am grateful to those who believe in me.

Walter Ball, my graduate school professor for my Master of Fine Arts (M.F.A.) studies, persisted in prompting me to discover my deeper self through my art.

Early in my professional career, René Mott, general manager of my employer's Peru operations, made time for me. He said everyone should write a book because we have a story to tell.

My mother's proclamation that I could do and be anything has lived in the background of my life. And my biggest fans, my sisters Deborah and Michele, reinforce that. They have awakened me to my fearlessness and won't take no for an answer in pursuing possibilities.

Contents

Part One: Embrace Unfinished

Chapter One	You're Not Supposed to Be Finished	3
Chapter Two	Achieving Clarity During Times of Uncertainty	14
Chapter Three	Your Bridge to Possibilities	35
Chapter Four	Awaken the Possibilities	46

Part Two: Get Out of Your Own Way

Chapter Five	Moments That Matter the Most	67
Chapter Six	Orange Barrels and Single Lanes	82
Chapter Seven	Bigger than You Think	97

Part Three: Unearth Your Superpowers

Chapter Eight	The Superpower Principle	119
Chapter Nine	Shifting Expectations	130
Chapter Ten	Small but Mighty	145

Part Four: Be Messy. Be You.

Chapter Eleven	Give up on Perfect	155
Chapter Twelve	Be Unfinished	164

End Notes 169

PART ONE
Embrace Unfinished

CHAPTER ONE

You're Not Supposed to Be Finished

> Open the window of your mind. Allow the fresh air, new lights and new truths to enter.
>
> —Amit Ray, Author, *Walking the Path of Compassion*

An unexpected realization occurred that day, twenty-five years ago, when I discovered I was living an unfinished life. It was my first visit to the therapist, which was a big deal. Being in the ninety's decade, I was not oblivious to the stigma attached to seeking help through therapy. My income was nominal then, so I was thankful that my doctor had referred me to a therapist who offered a sliding-scale fee. I was in my late twenties, busy working part-time, and trying to find my way as an artist. My husband and I had married young, three years after meeting when I was only nineteen and he was twenty-two. Life seemed pretty good.

In hindsight, I had been true to myself in so many ways, by living out my dreams of achieving both my bachelor's and master's degrees in fine arts by my mid-twenties. I wanted to teach art and envisioned myself being a professor. But this path did not come to fruition. These were the days before LinkedIn and social media, so I had mailed twenty packets across the country, including reference letters, personal statements, handwritten applications, and slides of my art. They were not PowerPoint slides but old-fashioned 35mm slides in white cardboard frames that slipped into those old carousel projector slots to be projected onto the wall. I can still recall the sound the projector made as it jerked the carousel forward. Not a single response came. I told myself I tried, and I moved on. Although teaching wasn't in the cards, I continued to explore my life as an artist, with my husband supporting my individuality and passions. I had a studio, created art, and showed my work in galleries.

We discussed having children from time to time, but my husband and I also considered not having them. We went back and forth for years. It wasn't only that raising children would be an enormous responsibility, but we would raise a human being, a contributor to society. What did that even mean? So many people were already in the world. What condition would the world be in for our child? Would there be an opportunity for her to thrive? What would be the state of the environment? And what if our child had a disability? For us, that was a lot to think about. So, we adopted a dog.

Macy, our Dalmatian, quickly became the love of our lives. Her former owners had abused and abandoned her before she joined our family. Many families participated in the trend that followed the live-action version of the *101 Dalmatians* movie. They eagerly purchased the adorable puppies without regard for their temperament and then gave them up after frustration turned into neglect. So many needed homes, so we gave Macy a home. She was untrained, and obedience school couldn't make up for what she hadn't received as a puppy. But

Macy was a lover who could not get close enough to us. Our house was hers—couch, bed, it didn't matter. She was part of our family, and we could tell she was grateful.

You're Never Done

After eight years of marriage and five years of Macy, we came back to discussing becoming parents of a little human being. We had an immense love for this furry being we had adopted from the shelter, and we knew we would have a colossal amount of love for any human being we created together. We were getting there, but we weren't quite ready, for many reasons. For me, it was less about finances and more about emotional readiness and a stable environment. We both worked retail jobs, which meant being away from home nights and weekends. Being physically present simultaneously for our child was important, so we made this a goal and gradually aligned our work to support our desired home life.

Around the same time, I came across an article that stated if you don't resolve your issues before having a child, you will just pass them along to them. This worried me. I was positive that I had issues, and I was afraid if I didn't address them, our child would have baggage. If I could repair or minimize some of my problems, my child might have a better life. Therapy became a precursor to pregnancy. During my first visit with the therapist, I shared my plan to set up my future child for success. It was uncomfortable as I disclosed deep, secret thoughts and feelings that I had never shared with anyone. However, I left every visit feeling edified and energized. Feeling heard in this way was something I hadn't experienced before. My most monumental revelation then, though, was that I was *unfinished* in life. I thought I had finished growing, but I hadn't. Why did I think that? I still had much to discover and explore.

I already felt exhausted entering my thirties. Prior to my therapy, I felt as though I had developed, explored, discovered, grown, and struggled as I constantly tried to figure out who I was and what I wanted out of life. I had felt tremendous pressure to choose a career and figure out how to be true to myself and become independent. As I entered my thirties, I had convinced myself that I had finished the seemingly endless process of figuring things out and experiencing uncertainty from the past decade. I believed that I should have been ready to move forward with a strong sense of who I was, confidence, and conviction.

That moment of clarification, when the therapist said, "You're never done," surprised me. Huh? Really? How disappointing. Looking back, I realize this was one of those pivotal moments in my life for which I'm grateful. If I hadn't made the conscious decision to talk to someone and work on myself, I may have gone through life being continually exhausted, dissatisfied, and disappointed.

Finding Meaning in Discontent

After the initial disappointment that I hadn't figured it all out, I felt relieved. And then came a new realization. I felt discontent, and I didn't know why, except that I knew it was bigger than getting ready to raise a potential child. It had to do with me and my pursuit of happiness. Like most people, I had lots of reasons for my angst, including childhood experiences, relationships, and current circumstances, which fueled my thoughts, feelings, and fragile self-esteem. When I was a teenager, my mother told me, "You hate everything." I denied and adamantly rejected it as a teenager, but now I knew it was true. I had an awakening. How could I position myself for success in the future if annoyance and disappointment were underlying my day-to-day emotions?

Our thoughts and feelings drive behaviors, which can become habits without us even realizing it. These behaviors and habits directly influence how we treat ourselves and others.

The results of our behaviors circle back to our thoughts and feelings, which may exacerbate unhelpful behaviors, and the cycle continues. Eckhart Tolle, spiritual teacher and author of *The Power of Now*, suggests that when you complain, you are positioning yourself as a victim.[1] That's what I did. I complained—a lot—about things I had no control over and others' actions, and I saw the world around me from a lens of resistance and depletion. I didn't yet realize I had a choice in the matter. Becoming aware of my thoughts and feelings helped me change them and stop the negative cycle.

Although I complained a lot, I also felt proud of my experiences and accomplishments, such as being the first in my family to earn a four-year college degree. My art was meaningful, and I taught ad hoc drawing classes in university settings. Also, I marched, advocated, and protested for others' rights, and I traveled. I was married to a loving and supportive husband who made me laugh. Although marriage had its own challenges, I never felt that I had to sacrifice my interests and passions.

How Do I Do Me?

Then I turned thirty. I was still seeing the therapist and continuing to work through my emotional challenges. And one day, out of nowhere, my husband said, "Do you plan on looking for a full-time job with a steady paycheck?" Ouch! It was a reasonable question, but it felt like a blow. Working full-time meant giving up art, but we were also ready to have a family, so that meant having more solid finances. *How do I reconcile this?* I wondered. I needed to find full-time professional work, which meant I had to sacrifice a core part of who I was—my creative side.

My husband didn't understand my artist soul. He couldn't because he was not an artist. I was a highly educated artist with lots of non-relevant part-time work behind me.

Through my art, I deepened my sense of self, which refers to what I knew about myself, my beliefs, and my core. My core was strong, I knew my strengths, and was clear about my purpose as an artist, despite many uncertainties. But now the future was completely unclear. What professional job could I secure that would align with my passions and values? Life felt ominously ambiguous for me, and my husband's fair question was a trigger for questioning my sense of self. If not an artist, then what?

Then one morning, what I hadn't seen became visible. I dragged myself out of bed, went to the bathroom, looked in the mirror, and the truth hit me hard. My life was not enjoyable. Although I felt accomplished, I was still unhappy. I wanted to feel better, lighter, and more enthusiastic about my days. Only *I* could change my life, and that realization ignited my desire for self-improvement. As I stared at the self-help section in the local bookstore, feelings of inadequacy visited me again. Admitting to needing help felt like a weakness, even in a bookstore. In hindsight, talking to a therapist and much reading helped me look at myself, gain perspective, reflect, and accept that a lifelong journey was ahead.

Only recently have I realized the power of embracing my unfinished life. I gained one other mind-blowing insight during that time. I felt lost in the space between my passion for art and sustaining and growing my marriage and potential family. Feeling qualified for nothing, I didn't fit into a nicely worded job description. One day, as I was going on and on about my angst, my sister looked at me with confusion and said, "Why wouldn't someone hire you? You have done so many things, and you're so versatile." She enlightened me about versatility being in demand by companies. I started believing it. It was life-changing, and that one shift in perspective reframed my thoughts and feelings from self-doubt to confidence!

Have you paid attention to the moments in your life when someone says exactly what you need to hear? Or have you brushed them off because of your stubborn attachment to unworthiness? I don't believe these moments are accidental. My sister's words on that day and in that moment influenced how I view myself to this day. They triggered a mindset shift from self-doubt to confidence, which refreshed my thoughts, feelings, and how I realized I could choose to show up in life. That one interaction and my response to it established a new foundational belief in myself, which led me to experience amazing opportunities that I might have missed. My self-talk continues to include the same questions. "Why wouldn't someone hire me?"

What if I would have rejected or resisted my sister's words? I started believing I could do almost anything, and I have had experiences I would not have had if I had not chosen to believe this about myself. Self-doubt creeps in from time to time, and comments, self-talk, or events test my confidence continuously. I am still growing, learning, discovering, exploring, and being, and I like it that way.

How does the concept of being unfinished sit with you so far? Does living an unfinished life feel threatening or scary? Or does the thought feel exciting and full of possibilities? What if living your life through an unfinished lens was an intentional design? Or are you counting on achieving a future state colored by your expectations and other people?

Try This

Take a minute and capture a couple of words in the space below—or in a journal—that describe *how you feel about living an unfinished life*. A life that is not about having it all figured out, reaching your highest potential, and achieving set expectations.

_____

_____

_____

Hidden Thread of Purpose

I have focused my life on people and helping them take steps to make it possible to become their best selves. I spent most of my career under the human resources umbrella, leading initiatives at companies focused on creating better experiences for both leaders and their teams. Whether the focus has been leadership development, overall learning and development, performance management, or talent management, my purpose has been to enable and sustain environments where people have meaningful, purposeful experiences at work and feel cared about, developed, supported, challenged, and inspired. It took me a while to recognize that positively affecting others has been the one constant in my unfinished life regardless of my age, job, the community in which I live, or the situation. It was my purpose as an artist and teacher during my twenties and in my interactions and relationships both in and outside of work.

My decades-long career in human resources in corporate America has offered variety and opportunities for which I'm grateful. I've worked in industries such as manufacturing, financial services, healthcare, and consulting, and in small to large global organizations. For my job, I've traveled to South America, Asia, Europe, and North America, where I've seen so much change, and that rate of change is accelerating. We cannot control many things that happen to and around us, and through it all, we long for *normal*. What does that even mean? The definition of normal is *typical*, but what typically happens is not always good. Normal might be an expectation that we cannot meet. Often, we don't understand change fully, and it is a mystery in which we don't know where we fit.

Change in us means being unfinished, and we tend not to like it. What words did you use in describing how you feel about being unfinished: stressed, frustrated, insecure, sad, unsure? Or does the thought of being unfinished feel liberating, bringing a sense of relief or elation that you don't have to fit into anyone's definition of normal?

You may or may not be someone who welcomes change and lives life with the ability to go with the flow. If you're like me and have a natural inclination to adapt, you still experience stress or anxiety during the *not knowing* phases of life, whether it be in the workplace or community, with your family, or by yourself. Your relationship with yourself and your unfinished life will influence how you think and feel, the words you say, and your behaviors, which will affect your relationship with others and your achievements.

Are you currently unemployed and looking for a new opportunity? Are you retired or nearing retirement? If you are in a relationship or married, are you experiencing bliss or conflict? Have you had a recent health scare or overcome one? Are you graduating college and uncertain or enthusiastic about your career path? Are you recently pregnant, or have you just adopted a child? Is your boss now younger than you? Have you recently found your partner or separated from them? Did you or are you downsizing your house? Are you moving into your first apartment?

What are you thinking and feeling during these changing times? These are all signs of being unfinished. Depending on the situation, you might be scared, anxious, excited, energized, optimistic, angry, relieved, or sad. If you are sad, is it becoming a barrier to interacting with others? If you are experiencing displeasure, are you operating from a distrustful lens? Do you have more energy because you are excited or enthusiastic? What you think and feel affects how you present yourself. How are you presenting yourself in your unfinished life?

A Kick in the Butt

Personally, I have been in the job market four times in fourteen years. Positions get eliminated, mergers happen, and organizations are sometimes not a good fit. Each time I find myself searching for my next opportunity, I experience financial worries, scarcity thinking, and feelings that I am not doing enough every day that I am unemployed. Each time I found myself in transition, I also experienced relief, knowing I was not in a place where I could be my best self. I needed that kick in the butt from the universe to move me from one place to another. Thank goodness I didn't consider myself done. If I had, then I wouldn't be where I am now, sharing my story and what I've learned with you. I'm still versatile, growing and learning something new about myself all the time. In each instance, I met new people who provided support beyond what I thought mere strangers would do. Each time I left my job, even when it wasn't my choice, I almost always found a better role with an incredible team, sometimes higher pay, and a better or more meaningful experience. Even the opportunities that didn't work out were necessary to clarify where I wanted to go next or where I didn't. Turns out that being unfinished has been good for me, prompting me to look inside more frequently to discover and align life with what is important to me. These are the moments of clarity.

Try This

Take some time to write in the space below—or in your own journal—how you feel when clarity *finally arrives* after a period of uncertainty.

_____

_____

_____

Small but Mighty

You might describe these moments in time as feeling relieved, lighter, hopeful, fulfilled, or clear. Between phases of being unfinished, there are incremental moments of success, confidence, progress, growth, learning, and clarity. The incremental moments may be tiny and not readily visible. In this world of wanting to achieve big, you may forget to pay attention to what I like to refer to as the *small but mighty*. The little things uplift us, make us smile, ignite pride, energize us, and give us the confidence to get through ambiguous times. Often, we let these small but mighty moments go unnoticed because we simply are not paying attention or because we think they are too tiny to be important. Without ambiguity, there are no moments of clarity. Without being unfinished, there are no moments of celebration. Not embracing your life as unfinished automatically places limitations on what's possible.

At my core is a desire to uplift others and enable them to be their best and true selves, whether at home, work, or in the community. I want this book to help you discover yourself as a force of authenticity, confidence, and purpose. Purpose doesn't have to be a big undertaking; rather, it is about being attached to your true Self. This is an undertaking by itself. The world needs you—there is only one you. When you are being true to yourself, you are serving your purpose, whatever that is. It's simple and not so simple. Being comfortable in your skin is the ticket to living with fulfillment during an unfinished life because you believe in limitless possibilities and know that the best is yet to come. Once you embrace your life as unfinished, it's never too late for most things, and nothing can stop you from achieving the next best thing.

CHAPTER TWO

Achieving Clarity During Times of Uncertainty

> You are possible.
>
> —Noom

In this chapter, we explore how living in a state of constant change can undermine your sense of self. I offer opportunities to strengthen your capacity to thrive in ever-changing and uncertain situations and environments instead of continuously questioning yourself and your value. You'll have some tools to establish your starting point.

Without feeling grounded during times of change and uncertainty, it's easy to experience stress, lack of motivation, anxiety, and depression which can even lead to physical illness. External factors often get in our way. When employees refer to company initiatives as *the flavor of the day*, within the sarcasm is a deeper feeling that their work doesn't matter. Have you worked for a company where your projects came to a screeching halt before you could feel any sense of accomplishment? We become skeptics of the companies we work for because before we can finish one initiative or even give it a chance, strategies and priorities change. We have a new leader, or a new merger or acquisition alters our course. Things just can't seem to get to the finish line because of perpetual challenges and changes.

Has *the flavor of the day* crept into your personal life too? Are you overwhelmed by brands, platforms, and services that promise to help you lose weight, get the best music, help you meditate, manage your finances, or look for a new job? Weight Watchers or Noom? Pandora or Spotify? LinkedIn or Indeed? One or both? What if I want a real person? In sifting through all the options, did you forget what you even needed?

Trying different things and experimenting are part of our unfinished lives, but how can you minimize distractions and build momentum on the journey to feeling fulfilled and accomplished? While multiple options represent personalization and choice, they can debilitate and interfere with achieving goals and desired outcomes. Continuously changing approaches creates barriers to feeling fulfilled, because we don't see the fruits of our efforts. When we don't experience a milestone, we might question ourselves, our talents, value, and sense of worth. We might not notice, but we deeply feel the missing sense of purpose. This waning sense of worthiness sets the stage for how we feel about ourselves in our jobs, with our families, and within our communities.

A Personal Renaissance

A few years ago, I received an invitation to join a small group of women professionals for self-reflection, self-appreciation, and personal growth. Synchronicity played a role for sure. The invitation to this group came when I needed the support. My husband and I had just moved from Wisconsin to Minnesota, out of a home in which we had lived for eighteen years, and our daughter was graduating from high school. We were leaving a huge part of our lives behind, including friendships and family. Our daughter was starting college, and my husband and I were going to have to figure out how to be with each other again. I had no job or network in Minnesota, and we didn't know where we would settle. The move was our choice, but it was also a time of multiple changes and lots of uncertainty for me personally and professionally.

When I received the phone call to participate in this personal-growth opportunity, I had no idea what the experience would uncover. There was a financial investment, and although I had a few months' monetary cushion, I didn't know how long it would take to find my next job. I was a little hesitant to spend the money, but I invested in myself. Little did I know I was about to embark on a journey to a deeper sense of self, self-acceptance, and increased confidence through reflection, visioning, meditation, listening, and peer support. The experience began a symbolic death and rebirth in my life. I experienced a personal renaissance.

It is easy to feel isolated in our personal life journeys, especially during the in-between periods when we can see what we've left behind but not what's in front of us. During these times, we can feel ungrounded, insecure, and even guarded. The women in this peer group were smart, educated, successful professionals who, like me, questioned themselves, experienced self-doubt, and were striving to be true to themselves. It was evidence that I wasn't alone, that none of us are alone on our continued journey in life. Some women in the group had lost a job, experienced a recent divorce, were seeking love and relationships, striving for better health and wellness, or had experienced a death in their family.

There is power in connection. We didn't know each other deeply, but we experienced a connection through the forum.

As we listened to and celebrated each other, we offered encouragement, laughed, cried, and grew together. Also, we created and discussed our future visions and talked about our pain. Collectively, we discovered how our individual historical experiences were a catalyst for what we valued and focused on. We were open to and didn't judge each other and were receptive to each other's unique being.

Pay attention to the following words, please. There is certainty within uncertainty. I believe this with my heart and soul. The certainty comes from your belief in *You* (belief in yourself). Don't give away your power. *You* can tap into your authentic self, regardless of what is happening around you. *You* are the only thing you can be 100% certain about every minute of every day. Regardless of how life and things around you change, your core, values, beliefs, talents, and authentic self are your North Star and guide.

How effective are you at being your true self at work, with your family, or in your community? To be honest, I'm over trying to fit in and worrying about who I am, what I say, and when and how I say it. Even as I write this, I know I need to remind myself of this often. It's odd how we need to put effort into being our true selves. We raise our children to fit into standards of behaviors and environments. For heaven's sake, don't color outside the lines. Although these standards might be a helpful guide, individuality often gets overlooked. No wonder being *You* can feel trying.

You may not realize that sometimes you have probably suppressed your own individuality for the sake of fitting into friendships, peer groups at work, and even your family. I remember a time not too long ago when I said to my daughter and husband, "I don't feel like I can be my true self in this family." These were moments of my unintentional resistance. I am curious and like to ask lots of questions. Because I enjoy talking about what I read and experience, I also like to share. Even when alone, I am a verbal processor and am annoying sometimes. I must balance how my behaviors impact others for sure, but there's nothing worse than feeling like you don't fit into your own family. It's easy to get caught in the adapting-to-others mode, but my goal is not to lose myself while doing so. In case you are wondering, fortunately, my loving family demonstrated appreciation for how I was feeling in that moment and showed me compassion instead of demonstrating defensiveness. It was up to me to honor my true self by letting them know how I was feeling.

My personal and ongoing development during my unfinished and continuous life journey is about realizing, leveraging, and loving my unique way of being and contributing to the world. This is a work in progress, and I promise I am not a perfect model. But this book offers simple ideas and practices that I have tried, some more successfully than others. I continue to strengthen my sense of self, and if you are open to it, you will continually move toward achieving the true *You* and a stronger sense of self regardless of your environment, circumstances, or situation. Recently, while scrolling LinkedIn, a post that shared the following caught my attention:

> "My 3 yo [sic] said goodnight to all of us tonight and then in the dark I heard her little voice say, 'Goodnight myself. I love you. (Pause) I love you too.'"

What a great way for a three-year-old to start her journey—loving herself. My first thought was how I should tell myself that every night.

You're Not Supposed to Fit In

In addition to pivotal people and moments in my life, a few resources have changed my life forever, in the best way possible. One of these resources was CliftonStrengths®, which champions the concept that every person has a unique set of

Achieving Clarity During Times of Uncertainty

talents, and when we leverage these talents with intention, they become a person's core strengths.[2] As part of becoming a CliftonStrengths® certified coach, I took the self-assessment to learn about my own natural talents. Claiming these talents and learning how they show up and interact with others and in various situations has positively guided my self-perception and self-worth. I'm clearer about who I am, which has helped me understand how I contribute to the world meaningfully. Learning about me and my natural talents was refreshing. It clarified what I sensed I was good at and why I reacted to certain situations in the way I did.

As of 2022, nearly twenty-nine million people had taken this assessment. Based on the data, Gallup found that, "In fact, the combinations of talents are so unique that the chance that two people share the same top five CliftonStrengths themes in the same order is an astonishing one in 33 million."[3] This blows me away because it shows how unique I am as an individual. And it shows how unique you are as an individual. No wonder I haven't always felt like I fit in. We aren't supposed to fit in.

The CliftonStrengths® assessment is available to everyone.[4] You will receive a report immediately after taking the assessment, which uncovers your top five natural talents. There are thirty-four talents assessed, and every person uses every talent, but the top five are the talents that show up the most for you naturally. When you are aware of these talents and leverage them intentionally, they become your strengths.

Humans like categorization and strive to turn chaos or disorder into order, grouping us by generation, race, ethnicity, gender, income level, education, job, and much more. These categories minimize our uniqueness, but I understand they also serve a purpose in many situations. For example, the world is trying to better meet the needs of populations related to healthcare and other services and therefore needs to have a better understanding of group or population characteristics.

However, I encourage you not to put yourself in a category or label yourself. Instead, use these tools to understand yourself better. Believe in *yourself* as an individual who has something authentic to offer the universe, your family, the company you work for, and your community.

Writing this, my first book, was scary. The path, outcome, and my capabilities are all unclear to me. Writing it has been an opportunity for me to question myself. *What do I have to offer that hasn't already been written? Why would anyone want to read my book?* While writing this book, a dear friend asked if I was worried about others having written similar content. What I learned through the writing process is that I'm the only me and the only one with my perspective and experiences. Through my book-writing support system, I became enlightened and felt encouraged when I was told that only I could write my book. Given the Gallup data I just shared, this is also rational. That only one in thirty-three million people have similar CliftonStrengths® assessment results are evidence to me that my story is unique. When discouraging voices in my head surface, and they do, I counter by exercising belief in myself and my unique manner of showing up in this life. I can count on *myself* in times of new experiences and uncertainty. So can you.

We and others impose many expectations on us to be smarter, better, kinder, prettier, slimmer, and fill in the blank. What we may not realize is that we are enough as we are. To encourage you to know and believe in your true Self, allow me to share some additional research that CliftonStrengths® has discovered and reported. When people have opportunities to leverage natural talents or strengths, they are "six times more likely to do what they do best every day" and "three times more likely to report having an excellent quality of life."

> Plus, "They're more likely to report having ample energy, feeling well-rested, being happy, smiling or laughing a lot,

learning something interesting, and being treated with respect. And they're less likely to report experiencing worry, stress, anger, sadness, or physical pain."[5]

For those of you who think these things come from lots of money, a job title, the next car, house, or achieving the expectations of the life we think we should experience, guess again. Isn't it nice to know that the surest way to be happy, energized, less stressed, and fulfilled is to know ourselves and leverage who we are? Living with fulfillment in an unfinished life of limitless possibilities is possible with a strong sense of self. What do you know about yourself? What type of person are you? Sounds easy. How much thought have you given this? Or is your idea of yourself dependent on others? This can be dangerous. Your idea about yourself is powerful and sets the stage for how you show up every day on your life journey. I have needed some guidance over time on my journey to being the best and most authentic Me, so I'm going to assume you won't mind a few suggestions either.

The Company You Keep

When my daughter was little, she came home from school and talked about the not-so-nice things the kids at school said to her. For example, in fourth grade, she was riding the bus home and one of her classmates asked her if she went to church. When she said no, she was told that people who don't go to church will go to hell. When she got off the bus and made her way into the house, she shared this with her dad and me. Lots of people, even those who participate in organized religion, don't regularly go to church. Our response was that this is her classmate's family's belief system, although it doesn't make it right for her to say something like that. My daughter, through our direction, gave this classmate the benefit of the doubt a few times, but when this type of behavior became a pattern, my daughter decided she needed space from her, and we supported that decision. When others treat us in a way that makes us question who we are, cause us to feel fear, or feel less than, it's time to move on. It's hard enough to reduce the frequent less-than-helpful chatter in our heads without others' discouraging contributions. I feel as if it has taken me a lifetime to realize I am enough as I am, and yet this continues to be tested.

My husband and I continuously challenged our daughter to distance herself from those who were not an uplifting presence and to surround herself with those who were elevating and contributed to her happiness and her ability to feel good about herself. This continues to be our guidance, even though she is an adult now. The group of women I referred to at the beginning of this chapter uplifted and energized, increased my confidence, and encouraged me to believe in myself.

With whom are you surrounding yourself? I am certain you have experienced how others' words, beliefs, and actions can influence—for better or worse—how you think about yourself. Have a look at those around you. Do they deplete your energy or fuel it? Are they encouraging and supportive or critical? Are they curious and good listeners or indifferent? As much as we don't want to depend on others to sustain our self-esteem, we are human and how others treat us matters; it impacts what we believe and how we feel.

Try This

Throughout this book, under the heading of "Try This," I will propose small but mighty actions and experiments in which you may participate for your own self-discovery, reflection, and adoption on your journey to a stronger sense of self. The more you opt in, the more practices you will have in your back pocket when you need them. Let's start.

- Take a few minutes to take stock of those who are most present in your life and write their names down in the chart that follows. Your list could include work peers, your boss, friends, family, partner, or community members and could represent physical or virtual presence.
- Assess each person's impact on you when you are in their presence using the following guidelines:

    a. Do you mostly feel criticized by this person or that they want to change you? Are you anxious in their presence or sense they have a minimal interest in you, your thoughts, ideas, or experiences? If you commonly have less than desired experiences with the individual, place a checkmark in the "depletes my energy" column.

    b. Do you mostly feel encouraged, supported, and accepted by this person? Are they genuinely curious about your thoughts, ideas, and experiences? If you commonly have positive experiences with the individual, place a checkmark in the "boosts my energy" column.

    c. Check the "neither depletes nor boosts my energy column if the impact is neutral, and it's also okay to check both the "depletes my energy" and "boosts my energy" columns related to one person.

- Then total the number of checkmarks at the bottom of each column. Pay particular attention to the number of checkmarks you made in the "depletes" versus "boosts" columns.

Name of person	Depletes my energy	Boosts my energy	Neither depletes nor boosts
Total per column			

Those who deplete your energy detract from your positive sense of self. *Healthline* describes sense of self as how you think of yourself, what you know about yourself including your core beliefs, talents, characteristics, and how you would describe yourself. Do you know your likes and dislikes and what motivates you? Your sense of self represents your individuality.[6] It sets the stage for how you show up and interact with others, and it can steer your motivation and amplify your self-talk on either end of the continuum. Those who boost your energy contribute to your positive sense of self. Although it is up to us to realize and embrace who we are as unique individuals and maintain our own sense of self, realizing the effect others have on us is a continuous and important aspect of our unfinished life journeys.

What decisions do you need to make based on your assessment of those surrounding you? Who consistently uplifts you, and how frequently are you with them? Who consistently feeds your insecurities and self-doubt and how frequently are they with you? No one is perfect, and I'm not suggesting you cut off people who are periodically insensitive and judgmental, as we all demonstrate these behaviors from time to time. However, if certain individuals consistently cause you to doubt yourself and your value, it's productive to think about whether you should continue to be in their presence at the same frequency. Alternatively, are you able to be honest with them about how you feel, as I was earlier with my family? They may or may not reflect on your feedback, but if they reflect, they may be more aware of their impact in the future. Is there anyone in the "depletes" column with whom you should deliberately decrease your interactions?

It is not easy to confront others, establish boundaries, or maintain a healthy distance—physical or emotional—from those you have allowed to injure your self-esteem, as it could be your partner, a lifelong friend, or a boss. You deserve to be your best self, and as much as you may want to change other people or believe you can, I think you know this is not possible. You owe yourself the truth, and I am telling you it is in your power to be the best *You*.

Try This

Refer to the names listed in both the "depletes my energy" and "boosts my energy" columns and complete the exercise below listing the names of one to two people whose presence in your life you would like to first increase and then decrease because of their impact on your energy or sense of self. You may include others here that you did not mention already, and you can complete this activity in more than one way. No right or wrong answers exist. Your way is the only way to go, and I intend this activity only to provide guidance for reflection and action.

- I would like to increase my interactions with _____. By (insert date) _____, I will reach out to them for ideas on how we can more frequently stay in touch.
- I would like to decrease my interactions with _____. I will create new boundaries to distance myself (if

possible) and spend less time with them physically or emotionally by

_____

_____

_____.

    I once had a boss who treated me poorly and was visibly spiteful and unkind. To this day, I don't know why. Her tone was disrespectful and disparaging. I had never experienced such unkindness and personal dislike, and I felt restricted from opportunities that would help me grow professionally. *Maybe it was me*, I thought, and wondered how I could improve the relationship. So many stories I told myself about the situation led to my shrinking sense of self and decreased confidence. One day, one of my team members and I were together in a meeting with this person. When we left the meeting, my colleague came into my office, closed the door, and shared how uncomfortable she was in the meeting because of how that boss had treated me. She couldn't believe it. Her remarks helped me realize I wasn't crazy, and I wasn't simply taking things personally. I could not be my best in this environment and knew I had to find a place where I felt valued and supported rather than suppressed.

    This boss was very present in my work life, and since I couldn't decrease my interactions with her, I knew I had to find a better environment. So, I began putting my resume together. As I began the process, my boss called me into her office to tell me the company eliminated my position. This was the kick in the butt that accelerated the action I needed to take to remove myself from an unhealthy situation where they depleted my energy and weakened my sense of self. The cherry on the top was how relieved I felt as I drove home in the middle of the afternoon. I had mixed feelings of course, but my primary reaction was relief—a burden had been lifted off my shoulders. Just thinking about something in a new way and taking the small action to refresh my resume invited something different, even if it wasn't my choice.

Our current self-perceptions root in deep psychological places and historical experiences, often from childhood. I am a believer in seeking therapy, and as I mentioned in Chapter One, I have sought it out and engaged in it. But I am not an educated clinician or your therapist. My intentions are to point out tangible actions you may take (or appreciate when someone takes them for you) to do something different to enhance your sense of self. Don't wait for things to change because they might not. You can make it happen.

How You Think about Yourself

Reflecting about who you spend your time with and how you feel when you are with them is a positive action to help you understand how others affect your thoughts and feelings about yourself. Let's take this to another level by encouraging you to build an awareness of how you think about yourself. What are the traits, beliefs, talents, or skills you emphasize as strengths? Or rather, do you de-emphasize or downplay your talents? In my career, while facilitating conversations with adult learners and asking them to describe their strengths and areas of development, the areas of development or weaknesses nearly always take the lead. We may not see or believe in our talents or don't want to toot our own horns. Regardless of why we downplay our strengths, this behavior will more than likely diminish one's positive sense of self.

While visiting my family, I spent some dedicated time with my niece and daughter together. They are both young adults experiencing and discovering themselves in their young twenties. We were in the car—where in my experience, great conversations take place—when my niece shared that earlier that week, a coworker told her she was patient.

The descriptor surprised her because she didn't think of herself in that way. My daughter then said someone called her friendly the other day, which was likewise surprising to her. Maybe they each were having an especially good day and the compliments were a one-time happening, but I doubt that. How many times have you given compliments to someone, and their response was, "Well, I don't know about that," or "oh, you're too nice"? How many times have you chosen not to accept a compliment or had difficulty receiving one?

What if we graciously received the positive comments, even if we didn't believe them? With the help of others, not even consciously trying to help, we receive words that can influence healthier self-talk and minimize our barriers to fulfillment. It's taken me a long time, and I continue to be uncomfortable sometimes, but now when people pay me a compliment, I simply try to say, "Thank you!"

Try This

It's best not to depend only on others' affirmations, but since they are an existing part of our environment, why not take them in and soak them up? I'm making the time and space for you right here and now to be aware of the words others express to you.

- As in the earlier depletes/boosts-energy-table activity, write in the table below the names of people—physically and virtually—who are most present in your life. It is okay to repeat and add names that come to mind. These may include colleagues, family members, community members, friends, and even your partner.
- Now, write the words and compliments you have heard these individuals use to describe you. Be sure to include both positive and less-than-desired references.

Achieving Clarity During Times of Uncertainty

Name of person	Words and compliments they used to describe me

Those surrounding us have a multitude of perspectives we are not privy to, especially when we are not living a conscious life. Sometimes this perspective comes as less-than-desirable insights, and other times it is absolutely affirming. Which insights do you take to heart more, dwell on, or believe more readily? If you are like me and many others, the less-than-desirable commentary most likely speaks the loudest. We judge ourselves most harshly. This can be noise and a distraction from maintaining a healthy sense of self.

Next, review the words and compliments you wrote. What surprises you? What themes or patterns do you notice? This reflection exercise is simply to raise awareness of your surroundings and determine whether those around you uplift or hinder your idea of yourself.

Try This

Refer to the words-and-compliments activity you just completed and take the following steps.

- Circle the words and compliments you believe about yourself and reflect on these words for a moment. Hopefully, most of them put a smile on your face. Some might be less-than-desirable but reasonable descriptors, and that's okay. Although these are not our focus right now, they may provide options for the ongoing growth that is part of your unfinished life journey.

- Cross out those you circled that are not productive or helpful, as these may be a catalyst for unhealthy self-doubt.
- Next, put a box around the words, phrases, or compliments others have shared with you, and that you believe to be untrue about yourself. If you put a box around the less-than-productive or desirable words, good for you! Did you enclose affirming and positive descriptors and compliments? This is important to note, especially if more than one person mentioned them. It is difficult to argue with themes.
- Use a highlighter to bring attention to these words and put a Post-it® Note at the top of the page so you can refer to it when you need a reminder. Why not accept these descriptors as true? This is one way to get out of your own way.

For those words, compliments, and descriptors you have a hard time believing, don't be afraid to ask the person who said the words for more details. For example, earlier in this chapter, I mentioned my niece received a compliment about her patience. If she doesn't see herself as patient, it's easy to dismiss this idea of herself altogether. Here's an idea to minimize the initial resistance to accepting a compliment. Tell the person who made the comment, "I appreciate your sharing that with me. What did I do that demonstrated patience?" This will help provide the evidence you need to believe something you didn't realize about yourself.

People, words, and environments matter. We react to the words and phrases others relay to us both verbally and via our devices as email or text messages. Although we cannot choose what people say to us, we can choose our responding thoughts, feelings, and subsequent behaviors. Although it doesn't always feel like it, we can and must choose our environments and those we surround ourselves with to support our ability to reflect healthily, celebrate, and show up with a strong and positive sense of self. Your self-perception—your idea of yourself—is what brings you clarity during times of uncertainty and ambiguity. The goal is to minimize the distractions or noise that prevent us from being the individual gifts we each are to this universe.

Your sense of self is how you would describe yourself in terms of characteristics, talents, beliefs, and values. We measure it by how well you know yourself and what's important to you, and it is a barometer for your thoughts and feelings, the decisions you make, and the behaviors you choose. It is what guides your life journey and potentially influences what you do for work and fun, where you live, who your friends are, and what interests and hobbies you have. What you think and know about yourself guides your responses and actions and influences even the simplest things, such as what you eat and how you dress. Your awareness of your sense of self is an avenue for clarity and acts as a personal compass.

Try This

Below this paragraph, you will see what I refer to as the sense-of-self continuum, which allows you to assess how you are feeling about your current sense of self. Would you be able to describe it to others confidently? Do you consciously leverage your gifts, strengths, values, and characteristics in your day-to-day decisions and throughout your life journey? Take a moment to contemplate how you feel about your sense of self and place an X on the line somewhere between *My sense of self is not clear at all* and *My sense of self is crystal clear* to represent your current state. The more clear, confident, and conscious you are about your sense of self, the more likely your mark will end up somewhere between the middle and the right end of the continuum. The less clear, confident, and conscious you are about your sense of self, your mark will end up somewhere between the middle and left end of the continuum.

My sense of self is 　　　　　　　　My sense of self is
not at all clear 　　　　　　　　　　crystal clear

The placement of the X represents a snapshot in time, and it could change from day to day or even moment to moment. However, the goal is a continuous and sustainable trend toward the right end of the continuum. The space between the current X and the right end of the continuum is what I'll refer to as your sense-of-self gap. We all have one, and as the title of this book references, this gap is an ongoing part of our unfinished life journey. Depending on where we are in our lives and the challenges or opportunities life throws our way, this gap might increase or decrease. The goal is to reduce the amount of time it takes to bounce back when someone or something tests our sense of self. And someone or something *will* test it.

Try This

Take a moment to write in the space below the names of those in your life who are genuine and brightening forces. In addition to those you have already identified in this chapter, you may also include the names of others you would like to be more present in your life because of the positive energy you feel when you're with them.

You can easily identify these because, in their presence, you instantly feel better about yourself, your day, and even the moment. They might come and go, but it's important to know who they are because they will contribute to a stronger, positive sense of self. By now, you are realizing how those surrounding you may either fuel or deplete your energy via their actions or words. Review the words, compliments, and people you just noted and go back to the sense-of-self continuum on which you placed an X. Hopefully, becoming more aware of the descriptors and people that already boost your energy helps to shift that X at least slightly more to the right. If so, make a new mark on the continuum to help you visibly see that you can quickly strengthen your sense of self simply by becoming more aware.

Summary

At the end of each chapter, I'll recap the key messages and small actions shared as bullets for you to reference easily and a synopsis of how you can take small but mighty actions on your journey to a stronger sense of self and more authentic and confident You.

- *Make and embrace connections that uplift you.* Surround yourself with people who uplift you, believe in you, and recognize your strengths.

- Life can be crazy and uncertain. Your sense of self, although a work in progress, is your rock amid uncertainty. *Strive to shift that X on the sense-of-self continuum* to the right by simply paying attention to the words and actions of those around you.
- It's time to *increase the space between you and those who feed your self-doubt,* deplete your confidence, and drain your energy. Boundaries can be difficult to establish, and it's hard enough to reduce the frequent and less-than-helpful chatter in our heads without others' discouraging contributions.
- *Believe the good stuff that others tell you.* Believe those outstanding and authentic words, phrases, and compliments. Write them down, ask for more details, and soak them up!
- *There is only one you.* Remember how unique you are as an individual. Even if you have similar characteristics to others, how they show up is unique to you.

CHAPTER THREE

Your Bridge to Possibilities

> You are an unfinished work in progress.
> One of the good things about life's challenges:
> You get to find out that you're capable of being
> far more than you ever thought possible.
>
> —Karen Salmansohn

My two sisters and I are close in age, about eighteen months apart. I'm in the middle. They are both tall and beautiful, and even when they are not their ideal weight, they look amazing. I am the cute one who inherited the short genes. When I do not keep my weight at a standard, I no longer look slim. That's just the way it is when the space between your hips and ribs, also called a waist, is about an inch. I am a t-shirt and jeans kind of gal. Even today, on any day when I'm not in my professional dress, I am wearing my favorite coffeehouse t-shirt and most worn, comfortable jeans.

We sisters have similar features and mannerisms. So when we are together, it's fun because people can tell we are sisters, and every once in a while, people wonder if we are triplets.

When I was in my twenties and with my sisters, I felt like the ugly duckling. I knew I wasn't ugly, but my insecurity grew and self-love dissipated when we went out to bars because they felt the need to dress me up in clothes and jewelry that I normally wouldn't wear. Their intentions were beautiful, but as I was trying to upgrade my appearance, I lost sight of the authentic me in the process before even leaving the house. I had fun while dancing and socializing, but this was not my thing and still isn't. I'm a homebody.

Spending time with my sisters is precious to me, and we have remained extremely close over the years. Hanging out in bars with them in our early twenties was depleting for me and only exacerbated my insecurities. For many women, attention received by men often feeds their sense of worth. Perhaps this is the same for men and for those who prefer same-sex partners. I wish this weren't the case, but it applied to me as well. When I think back about the guys who were hitting on my sisters and not me, it's not surprising since I strayed from my natural self before I left the apartment. I'm certain that a narrative formulated in my head that the real me wasn't worthy or deserving of attention, and I wasn't even aware of it. This self-talk ended up being the foundation for my night out.

What is the story you tell yourself, and how does this position you for whatever lies ahead? I hadn't yet done the work to identify my value and gifts in a way that fueled my sense of self. Looking back, I would have had a sizable gap on the sense-of-self continuum.

It Was Here All Along

During a recent virtual happy hour with my sisters, we triggered a memory and had a conversation about my graduate show in 1994, which was part of securing my master's degree in fine arts. The title of my show was *Sense of Self*. And here I am nearly thirty years later writing about sense of self. The drawings were life-sized figures of nude women, and my goal was to bring their strengths and powers to life on paper. The women I chose as subjects were friends, family (including my mom), and others with figures of all shapes and sizes. One woman was even eight months pregnant. Sometimes these women were strangers who saw and experienced my art in a gallery and wanted to be part of it. Each model's sense of self was present in her poses and through the shapes I formed via the relationship between myself, the mixed mediums I used, and the paper. I admired their comfort with themselves. They breathed it. I think this subject and the women who posed for the drawings drew me in because I lacked a sense of self.

My art was an opportunity to go deeper within myself unconsciously through this process. We are who we are and recognizing, defining, and refining our idea of our Self is an important part of narrowing our sense-of-self gap. Today, I find comfort in realizing I am—at my core—the same person I have always been, only better, more seasoned, experienced, and knowledgeable, and I know the best is yet to come. My sense-of-self journey has had and continues to have its own challenges, and I have had setbacks along the way. Situations, environments, mindsets, and the stories we tell ourselves can cause our setbacks.

Shift Your Story

Birth order has a stigma attached to it and science behind it. Growing up, I was aware of the less-than-positive traits of the middle child, and I felt left out, inadequate, and had low self-esteem. As a middle child, I have also detrimentally referred to myself as a people-pleaser, which I believe has gotten in the way of being my authentic self throughout my journey in life. Somewhere in the middle of my career, I asked a colleague, "Can you tell I am the middle child?" My colleague, who has her Ph.D. and is a clinician, responded,

"You mean the well-adjusted one?" She was serious. This is something I mentally noted and never forgot.

Previously, I only referenced the less-than-desirable traits of being the middle child, and after that conversation, I purchased a book about the middle child and read it from cover to cover to help me embrace my middle-child traits, which fueled my confidence rather than depleted it. I soaked it up and told myself another narrative. Research and science supported it, so I knew it was valid. Although I no longer have the book, with a quick search on Google, I again refreshed my story when I found favorable traits of the middle child in an online article that stated, "The middle child tends to be the family peace-keeper and often possesses traits like agreeableness and loyalty." The article further reported that

> "A 2010 review of birth order literature also found that it's common for middle children to be sociable, faithful in their relationships and good at relating to both older and younger people. Because middle children are often stuck in the middle, quite literally, they tend to be great negotiators and compromisers."[7]

It took me a few minutes to refresh my lens and enhance my narrative regarding my value and gifts, which immediately reduced my gap on the sense-of-self continuum.

Just as your life is unfinished, so is your self-narrative. Where would you place your X on your sense-of-self continuum at this moment? To the right or left of the middle? The placement of your X is your current state, and we also refer to it as your FROM. Where would you desire the X to be placed in the future, the place for which you are striving? This is your TO. To shift that X on the sense-of-self continuum sustainably, it is vital to build awareness of your FROM-TO story. What is your FROM state? What is the current story you are telling yourself and others about who you are? If your current story is less than helpful, how can you quickly shift your story to a more desirable state? Recognizing your FROM narrative is the first step in determining your TO narrative. The example I shared about my own view of myself as a middle child was one way for me to build a TO narrative quickly. It wasn't as easy as turning on a light switch, but the science-supported knowledge that middle children have positive attributes helped me see myself in a different light. This was the beginning of my journey to shifting the X on my personal sense-of-self continuum.

Unfinished Relationships

My husband and I have been married for over thirty years now. I am in denial about this. It's ridiculous how time flies. Plus, in my mind, I'm just not old enough to be married this long! Somewhere around our twenty-fifth year of marriage, I went to my doctor for my annual checkup. My doctor had been my physician for my whole adult life, so she knew me and had been there for me in both good and challenging times. I experienced her growth as much as she had experienced mine. Because annual well-check appointments are not solely about physical well-being, she asked about my relationship with my husband and how things were at home. My response, with a sarcastic tone because I was experiencing some relationship challenges then, was, "I've only thought about divorce seven or eight times over the past twenty-five years." Her reciprocated sarcastic response was, "That's all?" We laughed. I felt better and reminded myself that marriage and relationships, too, were unfinished, ongoing journeys.

When my relationship with my husband feels as though it is in disarray, it triggers a larger gap in my sense of self. Several years ago, during one of these challenging times, I saw a therapist again to help me work through some things. She recommended that my husband and I take an assessment to learn about our languages of love. If you aren't aware of the languages of love, you can check them out with a Google search and take the free assessment. The idea was to help us build awareness about how we each prefer to receive love. With this knowledge, if there was a willingness, we could better meet each other's needs by being more intentional and aware.

In the process, I learned something about myself. My number one language of love is *affirmation*. For those of you who depend on others to affirm your value and worth, this one's for you. The point of knowing this is two-fold. First, it's good for my partner to know that affirmation is how I feel loved. I can't help it. It's who I am. Bring on the compliments and recognition of the good stuff I do at home and at work. Tell me you like my cooking, thank me for doing the laundry, let me know I'm a great mom, give me hugs, and tell me I'm pretty. My husband's top language of love is *acts of service*. This makes so much sense to me. I rarely need to fill my gas tank. I love that, especially when it's ten degrees outside. He walked the dog early nearly every morning. Again, I love this when it's frigid outside, plus I am not a morning person. If we need something in the house, he's off to the grocery store, Walgreens, or Home Depot in a blink.

For me to show him love is to participate in acts of service that fill his bucket. When he comes home from a business trip, it's a pleasant feeling for him to come home to a cleaner house, so I usually try to pick things up a little. Cleaning is the thing I have the least motivation for, but it helps him feel less anxious when he walks in the door. I remember earlier in our marriage before I knew about the languages of love, we had a tiny house of about 850 square feet with a small bathroom, in which I left my hairdryer out every day. My husband found this very annoying and one day asked me if I could just put it away when I'm finished with it. So, I did. Simple. He was happy. Just to confirm, I'm not always good at remembering to show my love in this way, but this is something I try to remember to help fill his metaphorical gas tank.

Meeting Your Own Needs

The second point of knowing about the languages of love or any other self-assessment is that it is another vehicle for self-awareness. I didn't realize how much I had relied on affirmation, so much so that if I didn't receive it, the X on the sense-of-self continuum moved much further to the left. This is an example of how I get in my own way. People around me will not provide me with all the affirmation I want when I want it. Although it would be nice, I can't expect everyone to adapt to me, and I can't control others' reactions or responses. This was a significant discovery for me over the past several years.

I had a boss earlier in my career who was one of my best advocates. He was intuitive and knew what drove me. After a couple of years, he admitted he stopped by my office intentionally every few weeks to fill my bucket with genuine recognition of the good work I was doing. He knew this kept me engaged and productive. Smart. Affirmation still fills my bucket, builds my confidence, and confirms I add value and meaning. On-demand affirmation is not realistic, and I am working on reducing my dependency on it while increasing my ability to provide self-affirmation via my self-narrative to fuel my level of energy and maintain a robust sense of self. By now, I know my powers, and I am painfully aware of my sense-of-self struggles.

Sometimes, we minimize our own achievements. Do you celebrate your achievements, whether small or big? Or do you just move on to the next task or goal? When I graduated with my master's degree in fine arts, I remember how much pride, joy, and fulfillment I felt because of that achievement. The day after the graduation ceremony, I thought, *Okay, I have my masters. Now what?* I thought of it as only a moment in time and checked it off the list. That achievement took perseverance, courage, failures, resilience, numerous hours of effort and dedication, self-reflection, sometimes painful growth, and self-discovery. It was no small thing. I didn't honor the qualities that contributed to the achievement, and I didn't reflect on, realize, or appreciate the unique talents and strengths that I brought to life for the accomplishment. My continuous work is to accept my strengths, remind myself they exist, and recognize them—not with visible, tangible, and significant achievements, but every single day.

Try This

The effort it takes to self-reflect and build self-awareness might feel overwhelming, but it costs nothing and can only help you align with your truest Self. Start building your TO story with the following activity. Taking a few moments here will feed your self-talk powerfully and get you on the road to possibilities.

- Return to Chapter Two and review the amazing words and phrases others used to describe you. There is no time like the present to make a choice to believe them and believe in yourself. Regardless of where you placed your X on the sense-of-self continuum, these words can help you achieve your TO state and can be another guide in narrowing your sense-of-self gap.
- In the following "I am" column, write the desirable words or phrases that others have used to describe you, you have self-discovered, or you have gathered from other places like self-assessments.

If you need objective evidence or support to affirm this talent, then the "I believe this because" column might be worth completing as well. If someone sees something in you and they express it, it is their perception and their reality that makes it real. This is evidence that supports your I AM statement. If you completed an assessment, the results are real and support your I AM statement. I've included a couple of examples to get your wheels turning.

I am...	I believe this because...
Enough	I heard someone say there is no rating scale related to being enough. I love this insight.
Friendly	Someone told me I was friendly. I didn't previously see myself that way. Then I realized I've been talking to many people lately, and it has been adding joy to my days.

If the "I am" activity was difficult to accomplish because of your current situation or environment, personal hardship, feelings of depletion, or hopelessness, please give it another try. The positives might feel nonexistent and personal strengths and power might feel buried deep within, but they are there, and you can recognize them. If you answered *I am unhappy*, that is okay, and it is how you feel. This activity looks for the external support that can highlight positive aspects about yourself to offset feeling unhappy. You can be unhappy and be brilliant, patient, friendly, and whatever other words and compliments people used to describe you. We all need to recognize and soak up the good that others see in us when we don't see it for ourselves.

Give yourself as many reasons as it takes to accept the qualities that you have difficulty seeing in yourself. Reflecting is the foundation. Acceptance is the game-changer because once you believe in your powers, you get out of your own way without even thinking about it. This is how you create your TO narrative, which is the healthier vision of yourself. During all life's uncertainties, curveballs, and continually changing circumstances, this process is also an unfinished journey, but when unhelpful mind clutter sneaks into your head, your "I am" story comes in handy.

Come back to this chapter often to revisit your personal sense-of-self continuum. If you already placed an X on the continuum, you now have a benchmark for your current state or FROM narrative. Your sense of self can change from minute to minute, day to day, or at any time in your life based on your surroundings, including people, places, and situations. Your narrative is the bridge to a stronger sense of self. Refer to the *Try This* actions often along with the following summary to support your narrative.

Summary

- *Awaken yourself to your FROM narrative* as the first step in determining your TO. When you realize your current story is less than helpful, reflecting is the foundation for enriching your sense of self and helps to create your TO narrative—your healthier vision of yourself.

- *Find a reason to self-affirm when you need it.* This action will immediately fuel your energy and boost your positive sense of self. Although it's helpful when others

provide you with affirmation, you cannot expect to receive it on demand.
- *Honor the moments, qualities, actions, courage, failures, resilience, dedication, and perseverance* it took to attain an achievement, instead of only celebrating big successes. You don't have to wait for the big ones. There are thousands of worthy moments along the way.
- *Revisit your "I am" statements* regardless of whether you need them. Add new ones as you discover them.

CHAPTER FOUR

Awaken the Possibilities

If you want to awaken all of humanity, then awaken all of yourself. If you want to eliminate the suffering in the world, then eliminate all that is dark and negative in yourself. Truly, the greatest gift you have to give is that of your own transformation.

—Lao Tzu

Do you believe it yet? That the next best thing is just around the corner? If you're not there, do you want to believe it? If you are aiming for being done, you might miss out on that next best thing. The key is having the right mindset, and all it takes is embracing the space between now and any time in the future. Even in the space between today and tomorrow, something new and amazing can happen. The space between *is* the journey. It all starts with belief and acting on your new belief, and then sprinkled in is trust that the outcome is for your benefit. This chapter is going to get you started by helping you get out of your own way to feeling fulfilled at any point along the journey.

The quote at the start of this chapter crossed my path just when I needed it. It speaks volumes. One activity the women's roundtable prompted was creating a vision board, which I resisted initially, wondering whether this would be a good use of my time. We were to page through magazines and cut out images, including words, that drew us in. We didn't need to know why we chose the images. I also bristled at the thought of spending twelve dollars each on magazines that I would recycle after cutting out a few images and words. But I moved past my hesitance and surrendered to the assignment. After gathering all the images and words—there's no magic number—the next step was to arrange and glue them to a poster board, and then . . . observe our thoughts and feelings about what we had created.

It wasn't only the rule-follower in me that got me over the resistance but also my curiosity about what might happen if I just gave in to doing something new. I was so glad I spent the money on the magazines because the energy between my physical touch and senses was important during the process. And I enjoyed it so much I ended up leading the same activity with my two sisters and nieces over Zoom. If you feel like using an online search instead of magazines to find images, that's okay too. There is not only one way or a right way to accomplish this activity. Simply follow your intuition. I participated fully with an open mind, and the experience felt like a combination of meditation or deep presence and creative expression. The last piece of the exercise was for all the women to share their experiences of making the vision board and their thoughts about the meaning they found in the collage of images.

Are you open to allowing a deeper part of you to lead you to images and words for reasons that are not immediately clear? Arranging and discussing the images will prompt unexpected self-discovery. You won't know why you are choosing your images but trust that there is a reason they are calling you. Maybe you like the colors or the feeling of calm, hope, excitement, or love you experience while looking at them. Perhaps they represent something you desire or relate to a recent experience, place, or person. It turns out they are softly and subconsciously speaking to you.

That activity prompted many insights about myself and helped clarify some things that were important to me. As I was creating my second vision board, one image stood out from all the others. It was a butterfly in a clear jar that had a lid on it. I remember pointing it out to the group of women, saying, "I'm not sure what the butterfly is all about." When someone suggested the butterfly could be about transformation, that clicked, but it was not obvious to me. That's the power of connection with others. We are continuously transforming, which may involve suffering and eventual moments of joy, but always solidifying who we are and deepening our relationship with ourselves. The lid on the jar reflected my transformation waiting to happen and the coming moment when something new would unleash in me.

Try This

Consider finding a quiet space where you can spend 15-30 minutes at a time to work on your vision board. As images, words, or phrases attract you, be aware of your senses. What colors come to life? What sounds are you hearing? The cutting noise from the scissors? Are birds chirping or dogs barking? Do you feel peaceful or calm? Are you feeling melancholy, love, or excitement? Do the images or words awaken your sense of touch or taste? Are you feeling present?

The following are guidelines to bring your vision board to life. Enlist family members or friends to join you if you feel this could create a more meaningful experience for you.

1. Gather a poster board, glue stick, scissors, and several magazines.

2. Set time aside to dedicate to this activity. Give yourself a timeline.
3. Page through your magazines and cut out images that attract you.
4. Arrange the images on the poster board. There is no right or wrong way.
5. If you are part of a group, when vision boards are complete, provide the opportunity for each person to walk through their board. Allow the rest of the group to share their reactions.
6. If you are creating a vision board alone, take a little time to reflect consciously on what you are feeling, seeing, and discovering about yourself.
7. Lastly, hang it up where it is visible to you every day because it will continue to speak to you. And what better way is there to recognize and celebrate this achievement?

How often do you take time to build a relationship with yourself? You can only strengthen your sense of self—your idea and knowledge of yourself—if you take time to discover, explore, and embrace that deeper part of you, which I refer to as your Self. The vision board activity along with the other activities I have already recommended, and those ahead, will help you build a stronger relationship and connection with your Self. The quote at the beginning of this chapter speaks to me loudly. I know deeply now that every day I continue to awaken to the possibilities in myself. The lid has come off the butterfly jar, and I am transforming not into a different person but a better, stronger, more confident, self-accepting version of myself.

I promise that if you act, even if it's a tiny act, the gap in your sense-of-self continuum will continue to get narrower and narrower. The Oprah & Deepak 21-Day Meditation program drew me in and was an opportunity for me to act on meditation. I didn't finish the entire program, but it had an impact, and meditation is now something I'm embracing. The more I practice, the more it becomes less mysterious, more relevant, and achievable.

One of the most significant perspectives I want to impress upon you is that there is no such thing as one way of being or doing. Meditation is an example of this. There is only your way. In building a stronger relationship with yourself, you will uncover your way of being and doing, and you will feel lighter because of it. The ideas in this and other books are for your personal growth, and you should consider them guidelines and options. Act when something draws you in, piques your interest, or gives you a little jolt of energy. Monitor your self-judgment. I am the queen of self-judgment and can empathize with the temptation to partake in this unhealthy behavior. It can discourage you when you are trying something new, and your concern about whether you're doing it *correctly* distracts you.

Trying things and experimenting are part of living your unfinished life to its fullest. Adopting narrow expectations for what you are supposed to experience and the outcomes will prevent you from embracing your continuous journey. Keep an open mind and celebrate the smallest actions you take. It's a big deal! As you continue to act, you'll figure out through experience what works and brings you the best outcome. Tap into those uplifting people around you, such as those you identified in Chapter Two, but don't compare yourself to them because they are not you. You are on *your* unique path. Remember the flavor of the day concept and don't stretch yourself too thin or take on too much. Trying to pay attention to too many priorities is the opposite of focus and will not bring meaningful results.

Try This

Meditation used to be a complete mystery to me and seemed too far out there to embrace. For ten years, Eckert Tolle's book, *The Power of Now,* sat on my nightstand. I'd pick it up and try to read some, but it felt like he wrote in a foreign language. I set it down. There surely was a reason I had purchased it, but I just couldn't get into it. Now, I can look back and see it wasn't the right time. Then one day a couple of years ago, I picked it off my shelf, and it captivated me instantly. What I couldn't understand before I now comprehended with ease. That experience is a constant reminder to trust that I will intuitively know when to take the right action.

The book is about being present, and reading it demystified the concept behind meditation for me. I now understood being present in a more complete way. When we are present, we are fully in the moment. Time seems to stand still. The practice of being present can be challenging but when we are truly present for even a moment, it is impossible simultaneously to think about the past or the future. Thinking about the future is thinking about the unknown, which is uncertain and can cause anxiety. Thinking about the past can unsettle us because it's already done, and we can't change it. If you do even a little web-surfing, there are ample scientific studies about the benefits of meditation and how it can minimize stress, enhance awareness, reduce blood pressure, and improve sleep. According to an article on Earth.com, some types of meditation can also increase positive feelings and happiness.[8]

With my epiphany and a newfound openness, I embraced meditation. My journey to experience mindful presence—being fully aware in the moment—had begun. There is so much to learn about meditation, and I am proud of myself for resisting the need to become an expert or let the need to do it correctly distract me. I started with an app called *Head Space,* which offered a ten-day free trial, was practical, and felt more matter-of-fact and less spiritual, which I preferred. Then I came across the Oprah and Deepak Chopra 21-day experience. Surprisingly, I enjoyed the more spiritual approach, calming background sounds, the inspirational messages from Oprah and Deepak, and the accompanying centering thoughts and mantra. My meditation journey next led me to try daily guided meditations being offered live on Facebook, but my commitment to six a.m. meditation lasted just a few days. Self-judgment crept in but only for a moment.

My business and life coach, Susan K. Wehrley, encouraged me to tap into my gut and my mind's eye for intuitive guidance in decision-making. She called this her Gut Intelligence (GQ) process. Her process reminds us that our gut alerts us when we must pay attention. Because she knew that I was an artist, and therefore visual, she suspected that my intuition would come to me in a visual way. Susan reminded me that my mind's eye may come to me in a dream, a visual picture, or even words to guide me to what I needed to know, once I asked my intuition for help. Her methods were meaningful and relevant, and although I felt awkward and clumsy with this practice, I embraced and learned from the experience and continue to embrace the idea of being in tune with my gut as core to my decision-making process.

Each meditation method taught me that several ways can help you find presence. Each one builds upon existing knowledge and experience, which allows me to go deeper instead of feeling as if I'm starting over. I understand that meditation is *personal*—unique to everyone. Instead of only celebrating big moments of success, I can now appreciate and find joy in even tiny steps toward a goal. My comfort level has grown in knowing that I have many ways to meditate and participate in this unfinished journey called life. This is my journey and no one else's. This is your journey and no one else's. I now look at all my meditation experiences over the years as opportunities to be playful with presence rather than to achieve some ultimate state of being. Being consistent is not an expectation anymore; instead, the practice calls to me when I need it. During those times, meditation brings me a clearer head, slows down my heartbeat when I am feeling anxious, and reduces unhelpful self-talk that would otherwise impede a healthy sense of self. This back-pocket tool comes in handy on the journey to becoming my best self. No need to worry about not spending enough time with it or doing it correctly. Meditation's positive, real-life results inspire and motivate my practice.

Hidden Agendas

I have another book story. I love books. Even though I don't read as much as I would like, I enjoy the feeling books give me simply sitting on my bookshelf. There are small piles of books on my nightstand, bookshelf, or in boxes that I haven't read and may never read. That's okay with me. During occasional purging and minimizing episodes, I donate books, and I have hung on to certain books for whatever reason, like the *Power of Now*. I guess I knew on an unconscious level that these books would serve a purpose sometime. In 2007, my sister gave me a book by Deepak Chopra called *The Seven Spiritual Laws of Success*. She wrote an inscription, as she always does when she gifts me a book. It read, "May you get everything you want by appreciating everything you have." She doesn't even remember giving me that book or writing that note. I loved the message because she took the time to write it, but I didn't fully understand it until many years later when this book on my bookshelf attracted me, and I read it. Something was different about *me*, not the book.

When my sister wrote the inscription about appreciating everything I have, I intuitively knew she wasn't referring to physical or material things or even family or health; although, I am grateful for all these things. I believe she was referring to having an awareness of the not-so-obvious things, such as the deeper spiritual self, passions, and values. Also, she might have been referring to nature, the invisible energy around us, the universe—or what some call God—difficulties, lessons, and the present moments. I'm not even sure she knew this was what she meant, but knowing her now and her personal journey, her words may have come from this lens, even if unaware. If you haven't picked up *The Seven Spiritual Laws of Success*, jot it down on your books-to-read list.

The sixth of the seven spiritual laws of success, according to Deepak Chopra, is the Law of Detachment. The author shares, "Anything you want can be acquired through detachment, because detachment is based on the unquestioning belief in the power of your true Self."[9] Being detached creates an uncertainty in our lives that we want to resist. We become attached to physical things and ideas about how we think life should be, what we want to achieve, and how we want to be seen or thought of by others. When life doesn't align with our expectations, we may become disappointed, and feel as though we are not good enough or that we are missing out on something.

In the spirit of embracing your unfinished life, I challenge you to consider that the more concrete your thoughts are about how your life should be, the narrower your thinking, the more barriers, and the fewer possibilities. Deepak Chopra encourages all of us to "relinquish your attachment to the known, step into the unknown, and you will step into the field of possibilities."[10] This has been difficult for me to accept; I still struggle to let go and to trust fully in myself and in the possibilities. As a work in progress, I work on myself every day in small but mighty ways. And resultantly, I have noticed an ongoing incremental transformation (remember the butterfly?) that's visible to me as a stronger sense of self. I am learning to get out of my own way. I encourage you to get out of your own way, too, by "awakening all of you." Think small but mighty, clear your mind of clutter, and make room for possibilities. Continue to explore and learn about yourself so that you can receive the gift of transformation.

To My Surprise, Journaling Really Does Work

Journaling has been on the periphery during most of my life. I never doubted its benefits for others, but each time I tried, it felt unnatural, and the self-judgment related to never feeling I was doing it right led me to give it up before I had even started. I concluded it wasn't for me. Years later, I gave it another try. Just as with meditation, inconsistency is the name of the game for me. Maybe that's one way I feel in control. Some weeks, I journal a lot and other weeks not at all. This time, I approached journaling as a strategy to reduce mind-clutter by getting unhelpful thoughts or emotions out of my head and onto the paper, so I could look at them and try to replace them with something better. But I found something else going on during those journaling sessions.

A quick Google search led to an article about the benefits of journaling considered through a scientific lens. It seems journaling reduces stress, can decrease blood pressure, and improves the function of your liver. Really? Just as your liver processes everything organic you consume, journaling processes everything you consume emotionally. Journaling can enhance your immune system, increase your memory, and boost your mood and feelings of happiness.[11]

Do you want to practice stronger mindfulness, presence, perspective, and positively impact your general physical and overall emotional health? Try journaling. I was not expecting all those benefits, but what I know now is that I feel better and lighter when I journal. Journaling is also a good way to feel present, and you could experience it as meditation. This makes so much sense to me because while journaling, my focus is solely on transferring thoughts to paper, which provides an opportunity for me to appreciate and deal with emotions while building a deeper relationship with myself. The outcome for me is a stronger sense of self.

If you are not currently journaling and are interested in giving it a whirl, be sure to have compassion for yourself, lower your expectations, and don't give up just because it feels awkward or inconsistent. This discomfort is a necessary part of your unfinished journey. If you are always comfortable, then you are done, and being done is not only boring, but it lacks a sense of purpose, exploration, and discovery. Who wants to be done? Discomfort and awkwardness will come your way, even if you try to avoid them. You might as well go with the flow of life and embrace it rather than resist it. Be uncomfortable. Become a fan of awkwardness, which arises when you're in unfamiliar territory.

You've probably heard that practice no longer makes perfect. Well, it never did. No one is perfect, and nothing is perfect. Who wants perfect anyway? Perfect means you're done and then what? Practice makes *progress*. The article I shared above suggests that one line in a journal is a significant start. Celebrate that you opened yourself up, no matter how much you wrote in your journal or an electronic version. There is no expectation of the number of words you write, and a quick online search will lead you to guidelines and prompts to help you get started. I needed some help with how to start and gradually established an approach that works for me. If nothing much materializes, my go-to is making a list of what I'm grateful for first, and maybe that's all I do that day. It doesn't matter if the list doesn't change from day to day. That is often the case with me. Whatever pops into my head that I appreciated that day, I write. This is enough to focus my thoughts and deflect from life stressors for even a few moments. There's always something. You could journal about the last fight you had with someone, or a movie you recently watched, or even pull out some crayons and draw what you cannot express in words.

If I am journaling right before or after my meditation, I sometimes include meaningful messages I want to remember, a centering thought for the day, or even a mantra. My mantra could be something Deepak Chopra suggests or a quote by Eckhart Tolle such as, *I am the universe; I am enough* or simply *I am.* If you need ideas for mantras or centering thoughts, Google is a great resource. Sometimes I journal my intention for the day about how I'd like to show up that day. For example, *I will appreciate others' differences today; I intend to see the sunny side of things today;* or *I will control what I can control today.* My morning intention shapes how I will put my heart, mind, and hands to work on that day.

Another tool I found helpful is a concept I learned about called the Book of Awesome. Using it means you focus journaling on something good that happened during the day and was uplifting, filled your bucket, or boosted your energy, such as a compliment you received or a sense of achievement from finishing a project. Finally, simply writing about your full range of emotions during that day is a way of acknowledging and accepting yourself, which moves you along on that sense-of-self continuum.

Try This

You know the benefits, now try journaling! Be messy. Be inconsistent. There is no one way or right way so do it your way. Try out an approach from this chapter or from an online search and do it. Try some things and don't take it too seriously or set expectations that you cannot achieve. Remember, small and incremental is best. Start here:

- Today, I am grateful for:
  _____
  _____
  _____

- During the past week, something awesome happened that uplifted me:

  _____

  _____

  _____

- My intention for today is:

  _____

  _____

  _____

Small Steps

Another book that drew me in instantly was *One Small Step Can Change Your Life* by Robert Maurer, Ph.D. It includes a quote by Lao Tzu that reads, "A journey of a thousand miles must begin with the first step." So, every day is the first step to something. The author adapts a change-management business theory called Kaizen into a tool anyone can use for personal change. According to Kaizen, this means "taking small, comfortable steps towards improvement."[12] I have had a lifetime of experience with people inside and outside of companies, and in my various roles as leader, coach, colleague, friend, family member, or mentor, I have observed misalignment of desires, actions, and results. It's complicated, and there are many variables, but I have identified some patterns, including gaps in sense of self, unrealistic expectations, and too little celebration of the incremental achievements that can fuel energy, motivation, and inspiration to keep us going.

In this book, I have already shared many experiences, ideas, and actions with you, but they are merely stories and ideas if you don't do something with them. I recommend you look at each idea as an experiment to try, then objectively observe the outcome. An idea is passive until it's put into motion. Journaling or meditation might sound exhausting right now, and it might not be the right time to try it. If you're alert to a deeper voice within, you'll see the cue and act on it when the time is right. Just like when I finally picked up Eckhart Tolle's book and could magically comprehend what I couldn't years earlier. Being in talent development involves helping companies and people be and perform their best, but information without action is just information. In fact, research suggests we achieve nearly seventy percent of personal growth and development by applying and practicing what we know or have learned. Twenty percent comes from our interactions with others, especially those who uplift and influence us in a way that contributes to our sense of self and confidence to take a chance on something. Only ten percent comes from formal learning situations, like reading a book or attending a seminar, where we gain new knowledge or insights.[13] We can also learn best practices from others, get advice, and ask for helpful feedback. Your continued personal growth can be happenstance, and that's okay, too, but why not be deliberate and conscious on the journey?

Write It Down

Did you know the mere act of writing your goals significantly increases your chance of achieving them?[14] You probably have a lot on your mind, and all these thoughts and feelings impede your ability to focus. Writing things helps declutter your mind and minimize distractions. If some ideas resonate with you, prompted by this book or otherwise, write them and create a plan. Don't wait. Your plan doesn't have to be perfect. Below is an example of one of many versions of writing my plan.

[handwritten tracking chart with columns for Week of 1/13 through Week of 9/14, and rows for Practice categories: Meditation, Strength, Stretch, Cardio, Journal, with tally marks in cells]

Fancy, huh? My process is messy, but that's me. In this example, I had a column for every week of the year, and my goal was to practice each activity on the left a minimum of twice per week. I didn't know if it was too much or too little, but how would I know unless I experimented with it? Some activities I did more consistently than others, but I did stuff, and I felt good about that. This chart worked for me then; it might look different now. You may leverage or come up with a better tracking method. While writing this book, I also tracked the number of words I wrote weekly on a hand-drawn thermometer taped to my fridge. Sounds like grade school, I know, but I found it motivating every week to fill in the lines vertically with a red marker. It kept me focused because I could easily see my progress.

Find an Accountability Partner

We all need accountability. For the second draft of this book, I recruited a writing partner so we could hold each other accountable every week. To keep ourselves on track, we connected nearly every week to talk about our progress, challenges, and book content. Before adjourning, we each set an intention for what we wanted to achieve over the next week. I am also part of a writing group, members I can share progress with, ask for advice, and learn from. Remember the twenty percent of development and growth that comes from social engagement? We all need to feel part of a community and know that we share our journey with others, even though it belongs only to us. It's okay to adjust things along the way when you need more realistic expectations, for example, or new definitions of what success looks like.

Try This

Let's revisit your FROM-TO narrative and the sense-of-self continuum as a guide. Place an X on the line somewhere between *My sense of self is not clear at all* and *My sense of self is crystal clear*, then reflect on your sense of self today. Is it where you want it to be? If not, where would you like it to be? Has anything changed for you recently? Has your X moved to the right, the left, or stayed the same?

My sense of self is not at all clear

My sense of self is crystal clear

Reflect on the small experiment you just completed and the new one you're ready to conduct, then complete the following statements.

- My sense of self has increased recently based on the following practice:

    Experiment I tried:

    _____
    _____
    _____

Small but mighty action I took:

_____
_____
_____

People who helped me:

_____
_____
_____

- I plan to try the following experiment to strengthen my sense of self:

  Experiment I will try:

  _____
  _____
  _____

  Small but mighty action(s) I will take (what and when):

  _____
  _____
  _____

  People I will leverage for support:

  _____
  _____
  _____

This chapter will help you explore and take steps to strengthen your mindset, build your unquestioning belief in the power of *You*, and awaken the possibilities in your unfinished life. I sprinkled more *Try This* experiments throughout the book to help you continue your lifelong transformation into a stronger, more confident, self-accepting version of you.

Take a moment and review the summary of the key elements and experiments you can play around with for deepening your relationship with yourself, shifting your mindset, and taking small but mighty actions that help you get out of your own way.

Summary

- *Act.* Any tiny action to enhance your sense of self. You. Will. Feel. Good. Embrace the concept of small so you are realistic and then adjust as needed.
- *Experiment with small activities,* such as creating a vision board, meditation, or journaling, to build your capacity to experience presence, which will help steer you away from the uncertainties of the future or the stresses from the past for even a few moments at a time.
- *There is no right way* or one way to experience new things. There is your way. You will enjoy or even have fun trying things while taking the pressure off. This has helped me immensely!
- *Embrace uncertainty* and detach from the concrete, the specific, and the physical ideas of how you think life should be. Within the unknown lies limitless possibilities.
- *Try something else* if you are not feeling inspired or energized by the experiment. Don't question your lack of enthusiasm. When you hit upon the right experiment, you'll know when to push yourself. Try something else and then something else.
- *Stay connected with those who uplift* you and will share their experiences, best practices, advice, and inspiration.

Social interactivity provides twenty percent of your personal growth.
- *Make a plan,* even a messy one.
- *Be compassionate with yourself.* There is only practice and progress, not perfection.

PART TWO
Get Out of Your Own Way

CHAPTER FIVE

Moments That Matter the Most

> The beauty is in coming close.
> —from the movie *The Space Between*

Mindset is key to turning your sense of self into your rock. In this chapter, we'll talk about strengthening your new mindset through taking care of yourself in small but mighty ways that meet your unique needs. Leverage some ideas in this book or find your own ways to spend time with yourself. Build a healthy relationship with your Self to minimize the unhelpful chatter in your head. Get to know yourself in a way that helps you show up with confidence. Ready?

Can You Switch Lenses?

I spoke with a woman who suggested there is no such thing as self-actualization, defined as realizing one's full potential. I was both interested in the statement and resistant to what she was implying. The broad-brushed statement made me recall the many times I had heard people declare about someone else, "They have no common sense," which I view as an insensitive opinion. Saying someone doesn't have common sense insinuates that they are inept. Is there even such a thing as common sense? And because a belief is common doesn't make it correct or useful. I'm sure many examples come to mind about things that once were considered common sense that are now outdated and maybe even considered destructive. I share this to prompt you to wonder who we are to demand that others think the way we do. If we operate from the belief that every single person is an individual and each of us brings our own unique gifts to this world, how can we think others should know what we know?

After pondering the woman's statement about self-actualization, I realized I misunderstood her intention and decided she had a good point. Being conscious and aware of our strengths and talents is a good thing and something I am advocating for you to dig into more deeply. This awareness can help you show up with rising confidence and self-belief. However, her point might have been that thinking we have already self-actualized or already know our full potential is limiting. Have you ever surprised yourself and taken an action you never expected to take and then felt enlightened and proud because you didn't realize you had it in you? Or have you tried something new after mustering up courage you didn't think you had?

Early in my career, I worked for a couple of global organizations that offered lots of amazing travel experiences. My daughter and husband had never been out of the country until years later, and I always thought they were missing out on an opportunity to broaden how they see the world. Chile was a place I traveled to frequently, and I had a colleague who lived there, whom I still consider a friend. He offered his apartment in a little Chilean town on the coast. We planned a family vacation and spent a week in Chile immersing ourselves in uncomfortable situations where we didn't speak the language, didn't know what we were eating, and had to drive in uncharted territory with Spanish road signs. Scary. Thank goodness for my friend, who spent a few days with us, translating and playing tour guide. Then we were on our own, exploring, discovering, and expanding our horizons as a family.

I had never thought of myself as adventurous. I didn't need to run a marathon, bungee jump, or do any of those physical activities meant to push yourself to the brink. No thank you, and more power to those who strive to achieve these bucket-list items. But one day on our trip, our family took a drive and came across a sign that said *Canopy*. We stopped to learn more and discovered a zip line that went over the rushing waters coming from the top of the Andes Mountains as the snow melted from its peak. We bought two tickets—one for my husband and one for my daughter. They could go have fun, but I was out.

Do you know that feeling when you are in the space between things? In this case, it was space between my current non-adventurous view of myself (my FROM) and another possibility of how I could see myself (my TO version). As I watched my husband and daughter walk toward what I thought was a frightening activity, I started feeling unsettled and wondered whether I had made the right decision. My less-than-helpful self-talk focused on the fear. I had a little chat with my FROM self. *Argh*! I realized I would regret not joining in the experience of zip lining in the Andes Mountains across the rushing water. I continued feeling the discomfort of knowing that this opportunity may never come again. There was no choice now; we bought another ticket. I had surprised myself.

If I had stuck with the story that I didn't need that kind of adventure, I wouldn't have felt the adrenaline rush that came with that experience. I would have limited my possibilities had I not been present and aware. And I don't know exactly how taking that risk has affected my life since, but I know that experience broadened what I thought was possible for me and helped to narrow my sense-of-self gap. I felt proud and adventurous—for about ten minutes. Yes, I enjoyed the moment and the experience as I looked around at the wild water below, the plush trees beneath my feet, and the wind on my body as I zipped through the air. But I didn't need to label myself as adventurous or not. I figured I could be a little adventurous. I'm glad I did it. It transformed and broadened my idea of myself, and it was a stepping stone to my current best self. Thinking about it makes me feel lighter, happier, and more confident, and increases my appreciation for myself.

From this standpoint, complete self-actualization would mean you wouldn't continue to learn about and surprise yourself. Like in my younger days when I wrote off journaling because I thought it wasn't for me. But then journaling started calling to me, and my interest in it over the past couple of years has surprised me. I had closed my mind to it because I wasn't feeling it then. But that's not what I told myself. There's a difference between dismissing something and saving it for later. I told myself it wasn't for me, which means I had closed myself off to the possibility.

Self-actualization might be contrary to the idea of being unfinished if self-actualization were an outcome instead of a journey. It would mean there are no surprises, no self-discoveries, and no adventure. I hope you don't want to have yourself all figured out because there are possibilities you have no idea exist yet. Limitless possibilities come with new discoveries about yourself as well as the world around you, which appear only with a more open and less cluttered mind.

If You Don't Ask for What You Want...

Sometimes I have amazed myself and walked away with significant insights. Your unfinished journey is all about being a life student. My first role in the world of corporate learning was training coordinator, which was an entry-level position that I enjoyed, but it didn't satisfy me for long. This role expanded to consulting with business leaders, facilitating learning, developing curriculum, and leading others. If I had defined myself by my title at this company, I never would have grown beyond the tasks in my job description. Four years later, my title was the same, and my pay had risen slightly year over year. It became clear they were unlikely to promote me to a formal leadership role, and my job description wasn't going to change.

I had read somewhere that if you can't get a pay increase, ask for a better job title. So, I asked my boss how I could work toward achieving the assistant vice president title. Her surprise that I was interested in that title astounded me. I figured everyone wanted that title, and maybe they did, but they didn't ask how to get it. A year later, I got the title, after working for it of course. It made me proud. I had learned something important about myself—I could ask for what I wanted and maybe even get it.

There were two lessons here. First, I had to ask for what I wanted, which was scary. But I did it. I learned how to advocate for myself and didn't know I had it in me. I tell my daughter to advocate for herself, and I would tell you to advocate for yourself, but it frightened me to advocate for myself. Second, people couldn't read my mind. I assumed my boss had known what I wanted, but she didn't, or maybe she wasn't paying attention. It doesn't matter. This important lesson has followed me throughout my unfinished life journey.

Try asking for what you want. Easier said than done, you might think. You might even sweat at the thought of it. Other people can't read your mind and don't assume your boss knows what your professional goals are. Should they have asked? A good leader and mentor would, but it's up to you to take action and let people know what you want.

Have you ever noticed those times when what you've been talking about or paying attention to starts showing up? During a visit to Florida to see my sisters, I noticed someone driving a Tesla, a car I don't see much on the roads. After I had pointed it out to my sister and we discussed it, I started seeing it everywhere. Asking for what you want works the same way. As I mentioned previously, setting an intention, and better yet, writing it down, significantly increases the chance it will happen, as it did when I asked my boss about the assistant vice president title. Make your desires known to the universe, your network, friends, partner, boss, and anyone else who might be excited and support you. Magic happens.

Do you know what you want to ask for? You might need clarity on that once you think about it. Continuing to build a stronger relationship with your deeper Self helps. Start by noting what's most important to you. You might have to muster some courage to show up and ask for what you want. It can intimidate you, but what do you have to lose? All they can do is say no. Can you survive a no answer? Of course, you can. If you don't put it out there, you won't gain anything, and things will stay the same. Do you want the same?

Try This

Is there an interest you haven't pursued or something else you haven't asked for because you're waiting for someone to read your mind? Or maybe you've been afraid to ask. Have you recently advocated for yourself, even for something small? Take some time to think about your interests and desires. Maybe you feel you've earned a promotion or a raise, or you're ready for the love of your life to show up. Do you think it's time to go back to school or get a new job? Perhaps you need a vacation, better friends, a cleaner house, or your partner and kids to put the toilet seat down. What will it take to make your desires happen? How is your sense of self playing a role? Is it limiting or advancing your possibilities?

Take a few moments to write an interest or desire you would like to request. Then prepare to ask by exploring the prompts below. You don't have to do it exactly this way, but maybe you need a little framework to get started. I only want to nudge you to take time to reflect on how you can leverage *yourself* in the process and minimize distractions that impede achieving your desires.

- One of my current desires:

    _____
    _____
    _____

- The question I need to ask:

    _____
    _____
    _____

- My sense of self has been interfering with my achieving this in the following ways:

    _____
    _____
    _____

- My sense of self has helped in the following ways:

    _____
    _____
    _____

- I will try the following experiment to strengthen my sense of self to prepare to ask:

  _____
  _____
  _____

- Small but mighty actions I will take to build my confidence (what and when):

  _____
  _____
  _____

- People I will leverage for support:

  _____
  _____
  _____

The Power of Thoughts

How do you typically show up for any situation? Is your mind clear or full of distractions? How's your self-talk? Is it damaging or supportive? Analyzing the past is not about reliving moments. Instead, we can learn from our successes and think about how we might adjust in the future. Some time ago, I adopted a new way to think about feedback because of a suggestion to replace the term *feedback* with *feed forward*. This intrigued me. Feedback focuses on the past of course, and the past can't be changed. Feed forward explores what we might do differently in the future. It's forward-looking and a kinder approach for our self-esteem. *Brilliant!*

For example, instead of honing in on the many ways a presentation wasn't effective and hadn't achieved the result

I wanted, I could debrief to explore minor adjustments I could make to get a better result next time. Restating mistakes contributes to harmful mind chatter that widens the sense-of-self gap. It seems we often can't help but focus on mistakes, failures, and mishaps because we're worried about what others might think. *What was I thinking? That was dumb.* Ever berate yourself like this? We can easily get caught up in this kind of negative self-talk.

In one of my jobs, I repeated over and over to my boss that I didn't think I was meeting my expectations. Guess what? She ended up believing me too. It wasn't true, but I had created a self-fulfilling prophecy. Those thoughts, which I said aloud to others, influenced how I felt about the job, the company, and how I showed up each day. In her eyes, I had waning confidence, a shaky sense of self, and was uninspired and unsuccessful. It became a feedback loop. What I thought and how I felt influenced my behaviors and abilities to achieve, which intensified my feelings of insecurity and caused me to pull back on my performance even further. I had never felt this way before—incompetent. The working environment, which was unsatisfactory to begin with, contributed to this dynamic. The company discouraged ideas and individual uniqueness, and my bucket drained until it was empty. Each day, my desire to go to work lessened. I couldn't be myself, and that would not work because if I couldn't be me, I couldn't be my best. It was an unsustainable situation, but I was stuck, even paralyzed. My self-defeating thoughts and feelings swallowed me.

I'm grateful the company eliminated my position. It gave me no choice but to improve my situation by moving on to explore other things. I got it, though. Being let go was a gift, and for the first time in my life, I did not internalize someone else's inability to see my value. That was progress. I stayed neutral because I realized this situation was not solely about me. I wasn't incompetent or a failure, and I was enough. Although

I had some work to do to build up my confidence and shift my sense of self over to the right side of the continuum, the next possibility energized me. Also, I recalled my life coach Susan's words, "This or something better." It reminded me I was unfinished and had more possibilities ahead where I could soar.

Likely, you have been in situations where you could not be your true and best self and maybe even found yourself in that hamster wheel of insecurity. Over time, we may be in denial about how much we don't know about ourselves because we have had so many experiences. Life reminds me over and over that I continue to have much to learn. If I stop learning or stop believing I can continue to learn new things, my possibilities become stagnant. When you think you have it figured out, it's a good time to remind yourself that you don't. Now, I live my life knowing I don't have it all figured out. I don't want to have it all figured out. It's liberating to not need to feel you know everything. When I think I have mastered something, I feel good and proud about it, but then I am on to the next thing. I don't want to be a master of everything. What fun is that?

Think about your FROM state, which is your current state or a recent situation that didn't go the way you wanted. After my previous role at a different company had been eliminated, I preferred stability over being in the job market. It was natural to think the market was scarce, and we often view and judge things through the lens of scarcity instead of abundance. When I had interviewed for that role a year earlier, I believed jobs were scarce. My financial cushion was drying up, and because we recently moved to a new area, I didn't have an extensive network. So, I took the first position offered to me. I liked the company and its strategic priorities, and I believed it was on the right path and trying to do the right things for its employees and consumers. But there were red flags from the start. I saw them but brushed them aside because I focused on needing a job. They made a substantial offer, which made it easier to ignore the intuitive nudges that it would not work out. Objectively, it was a good role for me, although a year later, I had new things to reflect on.

Stop, Start, Continue

A great self-reflection tool is called Stop, Start, and Continue. Its framework helps you to analyze previous situations by identifying what you did well and could change in the future. It's a great *feed forward* model. In my example, my *Start* would be to honor my intuition. As early as the first interview, I ignored concerns because I was worried about my income. My *Stop* would be to stop believing I didn't deserve something better and that there was no other opportunity available. This can be challenging during uncertain times. You might relate to what went through my mind back then. *I don't want to disappoint my husband. I don't know how long it will take to find the right opportunity. This job pays so well, and I might not find another one that pays the same.* All kinds of thoughts can hijack our minds when we have a scarcity mindset. My *Continue* would be positive self-talk and strong support systems to provide the extra encouragement I needed to reset my belief in my Self and my talents during that uncertain time.

Try This

Try using the Start, Stop, and Continue tool to reflect upon a recent situation and explore potential scenarios that could trip you up. You will feel more in control and be able to move quicker on a plan to act instead of staying trapped in a paralyzing cycle of defeatist thoughts. Complete the following prompts to practice the *Start, Stop, and Continue* method to regenerate yourself. Leverage a situation you might have identified while reading earlier chapters or use something fresher in your mind.

- A recent situation I would like to reflect on is:

  _____

  _____

- In the future, I want to Stop_____

  _____

  because this approach, these words, or this action was not helpful or productive in getting to the intended outcome.
- I would like to Start_____

  _____

  because, upon reflection, I think it might be a more helpful and productive approach.
- I would love to Continue_____

  _____

  because it went well, I feel proud that I took this approach, it seemed to be helpful, and my intuition was right, etc.

Also, you need not complete this activity alone. You may enlist help from those around you who observed the situation, or a trustworthy confidante who will be candid and genuine because they care about you. I often tap into others, including colleagues, friends, and family members, who can help me think through or provide perspective about situations. Another thing to consider is using this model to analyze situations that ended well. Becoming conscious of why things go well is as important as focusing on improving your shortcomings. You'll be able to pull those competencies out quicker to get the result you want when you're more aware of them.

Presence and Thoughts

Being present does not mean we never think about the future and our place in it. We need to plan meals for the next week and determine how much to save for retirement. But being present helps us enjoy life in the moment. Eckhart Tolle held a series of brief conversations online about conscious manifestation. Each day, I discover the importance of this more and more. I see it for myself, and I want more of it. He says there is only the present and nothing else. Wrap your mind around that for a minute. We experience life in the present moment—always. We are living in this moment and need to make a choice to be here each moment.

When I was trying to comprehend this idea while listening to Tolle speak, my resistance took the form of judging him as a privileged wealthy guy. Then, as I listened more, this spiritual teacher shared his story, which included being suicidal, giving up, and then feeling liberation and joy as a homeless man. I cannot even imagine being in that place, but many people have been there. He appreciated life at that moment. Appreciating certain moments may be extremely difficult depending on the hardship, and I do not intend to minimize hardship. I have read other authors' stories about being able to be present during times of great suffering, which they credit with changing their lives. I cannot come close to imagining being in those situations, but I figure if these authors believe in the power of themselves and trust in themselves, then so can I, and so can you.

There is no time like the present to reflect on your daily presence honestly and candidly. In the previous chapter, you heard stories and learned concepts to strengthen your relationship with Self, which fuels your view of yourself and affects your mindset and thoughts. Your thoughts and feelings influence your actions, but *you* are not your thoughts—another mind-bender! I have heard this statement from therapists and many authors, including my two favorite spiritual leaders, Eckhart Tolle and Deepak Chopra. This is such a powerful statement. Our sense of self, or our idea of ourselves, derives from our thoughts. Each of us has over six-thousand thoughts going through our minds each day.[15] Our thoughts can clutter our minds and prevent us from being present and embracing an unfinished life of possibilities.

Next, we're going to identify and explore some of your personal obstacles, which will help lay more groundwork for living a life full of pleasant surprises, fulfillment, and gratification. First, let's recap a few items from this chapter to keep in mind or refer to at a glance.

Summary

- *Pay attention to the "space between"* during a situation and your potential response to it. See the moment through the lens of opportunity and possibility instead of being swallowed up by a scarcity mindset. The space between represents the middle of the FROM, which may come from the lens of fear, doubt, or "I can't" and the TO, which may result from looking through the lens of self-surprise, confidence, or "I can." Your self-talk will determine whether you stay in the FROM state or take a step towards possibility.

- *Try asking for what you want* and see what happens. Look at it as an experiment. Remember that people cannot read your mind, and when you voice your desires, they will be more likely to accommodate them. If you keep them to yourself, there is little possibility of them coming to life. Also, synchronicity is an amazing thing! Put those desires out there.

- *Take stock of your sense of self every day.* Where are you on the continuum, and how is your current state helping or impeding you?

- *Try the Stop, Start, and Continue* activity for a more objective and healthier way to move forward. Enlist the help of others who are trustworthy, willing to be honest, and authentic. Shift from focusing on past mistakes or undesirable outcomes to a present and future lens.
- *Continue to explore your own mindset* to positively fuel your sense of self. Accept the challenge to dig a little deeper into your experiences, leave room for continuous insights about yourself, and realize the value of surprise.

CHAPTER SIX

Orange Barrels and Single Lanes

> Some changes look negative on the surface but you will soon realize that space is being created in your life for something new to emerge.
>
> —Eckhart Tolle

At this point in the book, you probably are already more aware of your personal obstacles, self-talk, aspects of your working environment that don't bring out your best, and the space between your FROM and TO. Ready to dig deeper? Being honest about how you have been showing up in life is a great way to better understand your FROM state. Think of personal obstacles as those annoying orange barrels and single lanes that slow you down as you're trying to zip to your destination. At least you see road obstacles. This book and chapter are about making visible those inner and outer obstacles in life that are getting in the way without you knowing it. If you're open, I'll help you see what you couldn't see before and then guide you to lay the groundwork for removing those orange barrels one by one to open more lanes, which will broaden your path of possibilities.

Of the last fourteen years of my career, collectively I spent over two of them looking for a new job and, in most cases, not by choice. My ego took a hit, my family's finances suffered, and it humbled me in both good and bad ways. I got trapped in mini-cycles of self-doubt, and I felt intense anxiety about my future. But if not for all those months searching for work, I would have missed out on the reward of having opportunities to meet and learn from so many people. It's as if I were attending a business 101 course and, even more, a life course. What I learned most was to trust in the process, the universe, people, and myself, and that something better was around the corner. I describe it as taking that leap of faith I have heard so many others describe. You really have no choice but to trust in the process and believe the next best thing is just around the corner.

Community and Connection

Having a support team was critical to uplift me when I needed it, especially when I encountered people who couldn't empathize with my situation. Any money I received or had saved did little to quiet my feelings of incompetence, self-doubt, scarcity thinking, or the challenges to my belief system. Have you found yourself in danger of being swallowed up by feelings like that when things didn't go the way you planned?

People are amazing, and total strangers have been incredibly supportive. Not knowing anything about me, they referred me to others in their network whom they respected, who were also so gracious with their time and advice. Community and human connection are key during times of personal hardship. During those many months of connecting with people, I learned so much about entrepreneurial and disruptive businesses that are offering innovative products and services. I increased my network by hundreds of people, made new friends, and could help others, too, which positively affected my personal level of enjoyment and satisfaction.

Paying it forward is a wonderful feeling. People want to help; they do. Find your people. Even though it might not always seem like it, every ounce of connection adds personal value because it comes from the heart and genuine desire. During the job search process, I had to sift through lots of advice and information offered with the greatest intentions. Some of it applied to me, some didn't, and some went against my personal beliefs. "Only meet with employed people," some said. "Set up twenty-minute meetings," was a suggestion about networking. "Adjust your resume to align with each role you apply for." That was a helpful but exhausting tip. "Your LinkedIn photo makes you look older. You might want to change it" was interesting and, I assumed, well-intended. These are just a small sampling of advice I have received from others about my job search. When you're feeling insecure, you must be on guard to resist the temptation to compromise yourself.

This is not a book about searching for a job. I share this story as one example of many external disruptions that trigger negative self-talk, probably multiple times a day. These distractions can lead to an even larger gap on the sense-of-self continuum. Comments and advice from others may intensify feelings of inadequacy. Such self-talk is like the orange barrels we encounter on a trip. Our thoughts, feelings, and responses to them can create new obstacles. This construction can slow down or even halt our metaphorical journey between our FROM and TO states.

Our personal single lanes and orange barrels take the form of words, the environment in which we work and live, and thoughts and feelings that get in our way and slow down our journey to the next best destination. But they don't have to. It is possible to minimize them. The ideas in this book can help you reduce the orange barrels in your life and widen the possibility highway of fulfillment, opportunity, and happiness.

Does overthinking get in your way of acting? Does your inner dialogue torture you with judgments about whether you are doing enough or focusing on the right things? According to the experts, during my job search, I should have had ten networking meetings a week, reached out to ten people each day, had ten connections by ten in the morning, and sent update notes to those who had introduced me to others. Further, the *experts* say to stay visible, I should have actively included posts on LinkedIn, sent ongoing updates to those who made time to network and support me, and remembered to follow up with the companies where I applied for jobs. All super ideas, which I appreciated being aware of, but they are also exhausting just thinking about them now. Even more advice and opinions than anyone could implement are available, and they can be overwhelming. Feeling overwhelmed is an obstacle and can stop you from taking any action at all.

No one formula, idea, or approach works across the board, and as I continue to connect with myself, I learn what works for me through experimentation and the results I achieve. During my various job searches, I experimented and discovered what made sense to me. The stronger my relationship with myself, the more I know what works for me based on my values, beliefs, and uniqueness as an individual. Stay open to learning and listening and linger in the space between listening, processing, and acting. Sift through things and then act on what makes sense to you. If you are not feeling it, or worse, dread something, you won't be engaged in it and won't achieve the desired results. Since you are unfinished, you are not perfect. Don't expect perfection. Expect learning and incremental progress.

What's Your Right Decision?

It is easy for this world of too much to paralyze us. Too many options, too many choices, and too much thinking creates complexity. Complexity is an obstacle and impedes action. Listen to your intuition and how your body feels. What gives you energy and what feels depleting. The best idea in the world will not help if the thought of implementing it feels draining. While writing this book and simultaneously interviewing with companies, my network advised me to share that I'm writing a book because it would differentiate me from the crowd. Others suggested I not share this information because they might perceive me as arrogant. Who do I listen to, and if I don't take someone's advice, will they judge me? Will they think less of me if I don't use their ideas? Should I care if they do? What does that say about them? The bottom line is that one size does not fit all, and it depends on the situation. Trust yourself, and whatever the result, more clarity will follow.

One person I networked with embodies what some label as a super-networker. He offered to spend an hour with me, but I scheduled forty-five minutes, thinking I was being respectful of his time. While on the phone with him, he asked why I had only granted him forty-five minutes, and said I should let him determine the time he wanted to make for the conversation. I thought that was reasonable and adopted it as *feed forward* and an immediate *Start* action. This was a reminder that there is not only one way to approach life or a situation. Twenty minutes was not this super-networker's approach.

Much advice I have received and books I have read about the job-search process touch on a way of thinking or approaching something. There are multiple suggestions and solution methods, but there is only one of each of us, which means we listen to others AND to ourselves and do our best. One caution, though. Don't avoid experimenting with something because you are afraid of it. If you believe it is a worthwhile suggestion and opportunity, try it. You'll feel great about acting, and this will narrow your sense-of-self gap too. Even if you don't execute it perfectly, you will experience growth and progress.

The super-networker also suggested something very important in the last five minutes of our conversation that I thought about intently after we finished. When most others were telling me to narrow down how I was searching for my next adventure, he suggested I expand my horizons. The common thought was that it would be easier for people to help me with my search if I had details, such as the company's size, revenue, employee population, industry, and specific job titles. The networker viewed that as *narrowing* the possibilities. While the specifics might make it easier for others to help me in my search, the specifics were orange barrels that limited the possibilities for me. Expanding my horizons was also about recognizing my FROM-TO and making a shift FROM a need to find a job TO an opportunity to meet and learn from interesting people. I welcomed that refreshing thought process. So, as those around us offer opinions, we are not obligated to embrace and implement all or any of them. But keep in mind ideas for experimentation and expanding possibilities. If I went into the conversation with my super-networking friend not willing to learn something new or receive ideas, I wouldn't have received value from the conversation.

Rather than approaching networking as a task to find a job, I perceived it as an opportunity to meet and learn from interesting people, knowing that the paid opportunity would eventually come. I relaxed into the process and believed there was something to gain from it. After committing to my new Start action and being patient during the little time to shift my lens, I experienced an increase in conversations with recruiters and organizations. The correlation between relaxing into the process and the acceleration of results intrigued me.

I still had personal goals I worked to achieve every week, but ultimately, the shift in mindset added value. It made me grateful I could spend this part of my life meeting so many interesting and caring people. I embraced it, and it made sense for me as the unique individual I am. I'm also certain that I could not implement this idea the way this individual would, and that is okay. Have I mentioned there is more than one way to accomplish something? Just seeing if you're paying attention. There is only your way. So, when you receive and implement meaningful suggestions, ideas, and advice, your action does not have to mirror or have the same outcome as others.

Try This

Consider an upcoming activity, task, or situation that you're not excited about. Use the following prompts to assess your FROM state, the place between, and a potential TO state.

- An upcoming activity, task, or situation: _____
  _____

- Describe your FROM state to recognize how you might show up for the situation. How would you describe your energy? Are you feeling resistant? Is your sense of self helping or hindering? _____
  _____
  _____
  _____

- Shift your mindset to design your TO state by answering the following questions. What potential value can you find in the situation? What are the powers and strengths you can deliberately leverage? How will you grow in the situation? How can you manage your expectations? _____
  _____
  _____
  _____

- How would you describe the space between? What is your self-talk? Are you leaning more strongly toward the FROM or TO state? _____

_____

_____

_____

Know Your Powers and Strengths

During a conversation with a gentleman who was also in a job transition, he mentioned to me how he felt as if he had to redefine himself for each job posting and in networking conversations. I empathized with him and could feel the exhaustion of being required to spend time and energy repeatedly redefining yourself. How could you ever feel you were enough? Not feeling you are enough is an unhealthy state of mind and doesn't help you achieve anything. We can develop and grow in our beliefs more effectively by embracing our Self as opposed to trying to redefine our Self. This gentleman was who he was and there was something outstanding about that. You are You, and there is something exceptional about that too. Even if you have similar characteristics or qualities as others, these qualities show up differently in you.

I suggested to this networker that he consider getting to know himself and the powers and strengths that have brought value to every job and every situation in his life. I suggested he think about how he could leverage these strengths as his brand instead of trying to reinvent himself for specific job postings and organizations. Knowing your core powers and strengths is a requirement for a strong sense of self. Although the job descriptions change from company to company, how his unique qualities added value separated him from other candidates. It may or may not be a match for the organization, but wouldn't you rather be *You* consistently than feel as though you must continuously reinvent yourself to fit in somewhere? Being required to change yourself is a form of resisting *You*. This resistance is an energy sucker. Knowing and being *You* is an energy-booster and will help you find your sweet spot in life. The power of your sense of self is not only the key to a life of fulfillment for you and your well-being. It is also the key to a strong community, workplace, and family. Your faith and trust in yourself are the foundation for faith and trust in others.

The Power of And

In a prior job, a couple of colleagues had signed up for an Improv 101 class and asked me if I would be interested in joining them. I thought, *What the heck?* Okay, I was nervous, but this time, I spent little time in the space between feeling fear and embarking on what I viewed as another opportunity to face a fear. I said yes before I could change my mind. Once weekly classes were three hours over ten weeks. I am so proud of myself because I went way beyond my comfort zone. I signed up because I thought it might help me think a bit more quickly on my feet in life situations, especially at work. Unfortunately, my five-second delay still stands. Years ago, a boss told me in a light-hearted manner that I had a five-second delay. We laughed about this, but it was true, and he named it. I was glad he did because it helped me understand myself better. At times, when someone says something to me, I hear it, but it registers a few seconds later. My brain needs this brief time to process. So, I thought I could benefit from building improvisational muscle. I'm not sure I met that expectation, but this class is where I learned about the power of *AND*. *AND* is about acceptance. It is the opposite of resistance and implies openness. In improv, participants build on what the audience or comedian before them says. They accept the words, no matter what they are, as their improv foundation. It's a truly amazing concept and was life-changing for me.

A couple of years after completing the improv class, I was speaking to some colleagues in the diversity, equity, and inclusion department where I worked and noticed three-dimensional versions of the ampersand symbol on everyone's desks. It clicked with me immediately. At the core of inclusivity is the concept of *AND*. It is not only your way OR my way; it is your way *AND* my way. So, what am I getting at? Each one of us can be who we are. We can be competent *AND* continually grow and develop. We can make mistakes *AND* feel success. This is the beauty of being unfinished. We can be unfinished *AND* experience fulfillment, enjoyment, and happiness along the way and in the space between. I believe embracing the *AND* is one of the most powerful tools you can use to get out of your own way. It is the opposite of limiting and creates a lot of room for us all to be true to ourselves in this big world we share.

Revisiting Self

Let's take a moment again to revisit your sense-of-self continuum. After taking in and practicing the ideas and concepts presented so far, what have you tried and what were the results? Place an X on the continuum to represent your sense of self in this snapshot of time.

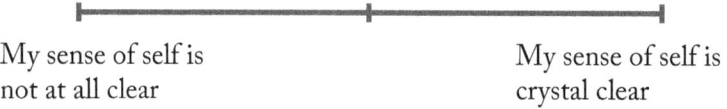

My sense of self is not at all clear   My sense of self is crystal clear

How do you feel about where you placed your X? What situations or interactions influenced where you placed your X? Where were you before? How would you describe the environment in which you live or work? What happened?

Who was with you? What was the outcome? How did you show up? What were you thinking and feeling—about yourself, others, and the situation? What was your self-talk like? How did these things influence how you showed up? Was this a moment that mattered to you?

Did how you showed up influence the outcome? Are you proud of how you showed up? If you are unsettled, which is a term I use for not feeling good about a situation or when I'm uncertain, this is probably not your desired state. No sense in dwelling on something that happened in the past, but observing how you showed up—how you thought, felt, and behaved—is a helpful exercise in getting to know yourself on a deeper level and building a more meaningful relationship with yourself. What outcome would you like next time? How are you impeding a better outcome? Let's refer to the "ways of getting in your own way" as the orange construction barrels and single lanes that I referenced earlier. Are you adding more orange barrels, or are you removing them on your life journey? Are you narrowing or widening your path of possibilities?

Try This

Right now, the goal is to recognize how you are impeding your progress by being aware of how you show up. Don't beat yourself up. Just observe and make a mental note. You can't get ahead of road construction unless you know it's there. Similarly, you can't get out of your own way unless you know how you're getting in your way. Right now, you are simply bringing attention to what is happening through self-reflection and awareness. Later, when you can pay more attention, you'll recognize and get ahead of it.

What in your life is represented by the orange barrels? In your work throughout this book, you have identified several situations for reference to define some of your common orange barrels. Some of my orange barrels have been my unhelpful self-talk, focus on not meeting expectations, not listening to or trusting my gut or how my body feels, and setting too many unrealistic expectations. It's time to name a few of your own orange construction barrels below.

Orange barrel #1_____
Orange barrel #2_____
Orange barrel #3_____

You are probably becoming more aware of those orange barrels. This is good. Know them so you can manage them. Some come from deep places, and they are ingrained, so don't expect to eliminate them quickly. The goal is to recognize them and eventually minimize them in a way that allows you to be your best *You*, regardless of who you're with or where you are.

Being Aware Reduces Orange Barrels

My husband and I have been together for my entire adult life. Relationships are wonderful, challenging, and unfinished. Whether intimate, friendship, family, or business-based, relationships are continuously developing because, as humans, *we* are continuously changing (not to say everyone develops at the same time or rate). Still, my relationship with my husband triggers me, and those triggers are usually about me, not him. I have learned that my reactionary and unhealthy responses have something to do with my thoughts and feelings about myself. Being reactionary is an example of an orange barrel, representing a burst of self-doubt and behaviors that may not make us proud.

On my path to being deliberate and intentional, I am learning to be aware of my thoughts and feelings and how they influence my reactions and subsequent behaviors. I realize these reactions result from my sense of self in each moment. I know the sense-of-self gap may widen or narrow, depending upon what others say to me, including my husband, friends, co-workers, and especially family. Can you recognize these moments for yourself, those times when you have reacted irrationally to others' words, actions, or behaviors?

Have you ever shared your thoughts in a group setting and immediately regretted it? Did you wonder what others thought about you or your comments? Did you think what you shared was dumb and wished you said something different or nothing at all? During my life journey, I have spent a lot of time questioning myself and worrying about what others think of me. This has also been one of my orange barrels. It's an exhausting way to live your life. I still worry about what others think but not nearly to the same extent as in my past. I'm progressing. The more I discover about my *Self*, align with my *Self*, and intentionally live as my true *Self*, the less I worry. The more present, grateful, and authentic I am, the more confident and fulfilled I feel.

Try This

How often do you say, "I should have?" If it were possible, I would eliminate the word *should* from the dictionary altogether. It is an orange barrel. It's hard to imagine how three short words—I should have—can be an obstacle to living our best selves. But, for many of us, they are. *Should* causes doubt. It makes us question ourselves and practice self-torture. Try paying attention to how many times you say "should have" over a handful of days. Tally them up here, on your phone, or on a sticky note each day. Eliminate them little by little. See if your count decreases once you are alert to them.

Day 1_____
Day 2_____
Day 3_____
Day 4_____
Day 5_____

You cannot change what's done. It's impossible, so why focus on what you should have done? *Should have* wishes your history away. Reflection is healthy; it doesn't wish your previous actions away but builds upon them to contribute to your future. Without those past actions, you wouldn't have learned or grown to be the best version of your *Self*. What happened in the past is necessary, and the intentional elimination of these three small words will immediately narrow your sense-of-self gap at least a little.

I discovered I have the power to question my unhelpful thinking and habits, and you have that same power. You are likely not conscious of these things and won't be until you become more present, which is why taking the time to build a more immersive relationship with yourself is vital. It is within your power to know and embrace *You*, the good, weird, quirky, strong, talented, and one-of-a-kind you.

Summary

- *Take a leap of faith by trusting* the universe and people, and believing things will eventually work out. Lean on your support system to uplift you and keep the wind in your sail.
- *Take stock of your orange barrels and single lanes.* They may come as words, environment, thoughts, and feelings. Plan to minimize these distractions or obstacles on your path to achieving your next best.
- *Trust yourself.* Go with the flow of your energy and expand your possibilities; don't limit them. Life is not one-size-fits-all.
- *Consider the AND.* Rather than rejecting, ignoring, doubting, minimizing, or pushing aside what is or what was, honor it, accept it, build from it, and use it as a jumping-off point to the next goal.

- *Eliminate the words "I should have."* It helps nothing, and everything leading up to this moment is necessary, is learning, is useful, and it simply *is*.

CHAPTER SEVEN

Bigger than You Think

> I don't shine if you don't shine.
> —"Read My Mind," *The Killers*

This book has posed reflection questions, shared stories to bring concepts to life, and suggested various experiments to try, all to help you develop a strong foothold when your sense of self is being tested. If you tried even something minor, good for you! Give yourself a pat on the back and celebrate, even if it didn't go perfectly. You did *something*! How did you feel trying something new—uncomfortable, awkward, uncertain? Did you worry about whether you were doing it correctly? Did you remind yourself that unless you are performing surgery, flying a plane, or some other activity that requires exactness, there is not only one way to do anything? There are as many ways to accomplish something as there are people. The continuous journey of our unfinished life is a series of experiments from which we grow and develop into the person we are.

It seems easier to support and help others than to do so for ourselves. I have taught countless individuals how to use resumes to express their best selves, but when it comes time to update my own, I find it paralyzing. It's easy for me to coach others but difficult to apply the concepts to myself. If you haven't experimented recently with something challenging that could enhance your sense of Self, there is no time like the present. Even if you haven't yet tried any of the ideas in this book, that you are reading it is an action and is influencing your future. You made it to Chapter Seven. You can't go back now. Let's keep going. You'll know when the time is right to take action.

Finding Your Inner Motivation

At thirty-nine, I went to the doctor for my annual well-being appointment. My daughter was about six years old, and I had never lost all my pregnancy weight. In fact, I had put on an extra few pounds while working for a global company. My job included frequent travel, which contributed to my decline in healthy and balanced eating. I also enjoyed experiencing the local culture through food. When in Rome, do as the Romans do, as they say. On these work trips, I ate and drank with colleagues who also became friends and teammates. My trips to China were different because I struggled with chopsticks. Servers sometimes brought me a fork when they spotted me struggling so I wouldn't starve or continue to embarrass myself. There was no chance of gaining weight there.

That trip to the doctor, coupled with my life then, triggered something for me. That was the year to muster up the courage to ask my doctor whether I was overweight. She kindly replied, "Maybe just five pounds." I knew what the answer would be, and I was grateful for the softness of her answer. That was it. If my doctor said it, then it had to be true. Suddenly, I was determined to feel like I was in the best shape of my life. I saw a nutritionist for twelve weeks, developed a new relationship with food, and became more active. And my nutritionist gave me homework and new habits to build.

Tracking what I ate for three months in a food journal was one of my assignments. I used the *Calorie King* book—this was back before apps—and it focused on recording my daily calories, fiber, and protein. My nutritionist provided calorie guidelines, and my discovery that I didn't need all the food I was eating struck me. I lost twenty pounds, and I'm pleased that I've kept it off. From time to time, I need to reset a bit, but I changed my lifestyle, and that's what made the difference.

Why did I start just before the Thanksgiving holiday? *No time like the present*, I thought. If I had thought about it too much, I would have procrastinated. At forty, I indeed thought I was in the best physical shape of my life and felt great. I set an intention, acted on it, and felt proud of myself. Along the way, I learned a lot about myself, my personal motivators, my challenges, and most importantly, that I was resilient. Regardless of whether you have acted yet, you are still learning about yourself every day.

Try This

In the spirit of continuing to get to know yourself better, take a minute to write what you've learned about yourself over the past few weeks as it relates to the concepts in this book. Are you becoming clearer, more confident, and aware of your sense of self?

- Over the past few weeks, I have taken the following small actions or steps:
  _____
  _____
  _____

- I have recognized the following affirming and positive attributes, talents, and strengths in myself:

_____

_____

_____

Now, take a moment to breathe in deeply and exhale, and just feel good about *You* and your awesome *Self*. Soak it up.

It would be so great to feel comfortable in our skin, not question ourselves, and always feel confident, but this is not possible in an unfinished life. Growing, stretching, learning, discovering, and sometimes being surprised by our own capabilities, talents, and possibilities are the outcomes of risking feeling uncomfortable. If we don't challenge our sense of self and comfort, it's not possible to grow beyond today. It is so important to continue to give yourself the gift of self-affirmation, self-appreciation, self-reflection, self-acceptance, and self-focus. Your ability to enhance and maintain your sense of self depends on it.

Fear and resistance to feeling uncomfortable act as an invitation for orange barrels to take up space in our minds and lives. Orange barrels create the narrowest of lanes, preventing us from obtaining even the smallest progress. Resistance to being aware and trying something different is equivalent to pushing aside possibilities. My husband reminds me often of the quote, "Insanity is doing the same thing over and over again and expecting different results." Fear contributes to resistance. Find your power by finding your inner motivation and minimizing fear, resistance, and the orange barrels.

When my daughter was nearing puberty, we had a conversation about deodorant. She didn't want to grow up and resisted it at first. On her sixth birthday, she cried, and when her dad and I asked her what was wrong, she said in tears, "I miss the good old days when I was five." My husband

and I chuckled inside, but we knew she was serious. As she avoided growing up, she resisted doing new things, like wearing deodorant. She refused. I asked her if she had a classmate that the other kids thought was kind of smelly. She didn't even hesitate and replied, "Yes." I continued, "You don't want to be that kid." From that day on, she stopped resisting and used deodorant. Not wanting to smell like that kid motivated her. We all need our inner motivation.

My daughter is now a young adult, and when we are together, we take a lot of walks. On one of our walks, we were talking about her height. She's taller than I am by nearly six inches. We recalled a time back in seventh grade when her goal was to be tall. I found this to be an interesting goal because I'm not sure how anyone can control their height. But together, we did some online research and found some ideas to help her grow as tall as possible. The suggestions included taking vitamins, getting adequate sleep, and healthy eating. Pretty simple ideas but difficult things to persuade her to do previously. Like magic, she began taking her vitamins, getting to bed early, and eating healthier foods without her parents having to beg. Her inner motivation to be tall compelled her to change many habits. And they've stuck.

In my mid-thirties, a program called Future Milwaukee accepted me. The program focused on building community leadership skills. It was an amazing and awakening experience. The participants were intentionally diverse in race, gender, and geography representing the city and county of Milwaukee and its surrounding suburbs. We worked with community organizations on meaningful projects that had real impact and outcomes.

The curriculum included developing a personal mission statement. Expressing my life's purpose in a sentence or two proved difficult but was also one of the most meaningful activities I've done. It changed my life. I quickly realized how having a personal mission influenced my thoughts, interactions, and behaviors each day. Twenty years ago, my personal mission was to positively impact others through daily interactions. It became very real for me when I wrote it down. And it hasn't changed over the years. It continues to provide clarity during times of uncertainty about what is still important to me. My personal mission continues to contribute to a stronger sense of self or idea of myself. It still drives my actions. The core part of my mission—having a positive influence on others—remains the core motivation in my life. It helps guide my actions, decisions, and surroundings. When I'm slow to realize on my own that the current situation is not aligning with my core purpose, when I can no longer be my true and best self, the universe seems to orchestrate events that prod me along on my path.

My daughter's internal motivation has grown beyond not being smelly and being tall. It has been amazing to watch her find her purpose as a young adult. It steers her interests, the work that attracts her, and the activities in which she participates. Over time, although my purpose and mission continue to drive my actions, my internal motivation develops too. Being my best Self and bringing out the best in others is just a deeper version of what has always motivated me. What's your motivation, and how can you leverage it to focus on developing a strong sense of self and embrace your life as unfinished and full of unlimited possibilities?

Try This

Take a whirl at creating your personal mission statement. An online search will bring up many resources and prompts. The previous chapters have helped you prepare for this activity. Glance back at the activities you completed along the way to help you answer the prompts below. To write a personal mission statement, you need to get to know yourself more deeply, and hopefully, you are on the path to accomplishing this.

Knowing what you value is part of it. Is it material things, relationships, achievements, community?

If it helps, research values, and from the list, choose five that resonate with you most. What successes are you most proud of? Your successes result from your talents, hard work, and passions. What are your talents? Where do you most like to contribute? To which activities does your energy naturally flow? How do you like to spend your time? What are you most proud of? How would you describe your personal characteristics and attributes? These are all questions that can help you determine your personal mission statement.

Take a few moments to respond to the following prompts and then create a brief sentence that includes the essence of the collective words. It doesn't have to be perfect. Remember, we are looking for the smallest of actions and progress, not perfection. If you struggle to answer these questions, enlist the help of others who will genuinely help you think through what they have observed in you.

- Successes I'm most proud of:_____
  _____
  _____

- My talents and strengths include:_____
  _____
  _____

- I'm most attracted to the following activities:_____
  _____
  _____

- My best characteristics are:_____

_____

_____

- My top 3-5 values are:_____

_____

_____

- My personal mission statement is:_____

_____

_____

Mark this page so you can revisit what drives you and where you should align your behaviors and actions. Your personal mission statement is a statement reflecting your purpose. It is a reminder of where you should or may want to direct your energy every day. This is helpful in a fast-changing and ambiguous world. Since my purpose has always been to positively impact people and help them be their true and best selves, it makes sense that I have spent the bulk of my career in talent management and development roles working in human resources. Working in fields such as information technology, accounting, or other jobs less focused on people would not engage me in the same way, nor feel fulfilling. People-focused work found me.

Not ready yet? If you skipped this activity, consider this a little nudge to embrace it. Don't overthink it. Remember there is not only one way to achieve this. Don't have any expectations; instead, be curious and open to learning more about yourself and what's important to you. We never finish self-discovery and reflection, and practicing activities in this book will help you maintain a sense of self that sits on the right side of the continuum.

Self-Awareness Leads to Compassion for Self and Others

Generalization about groups of people who co-exist with us in the world is a common occurrence, along with judgment and a lack of curiosity, especially regarding those who are different and think differently. Some of us resist the idea that all people have unique gifts that could benefit this world. We are all unique individuals, and in seeking acceptance and appreciation from others, we must offer the same acceptance and appreciation to them. Who are we to minimize and devalue the existence of others or rank ourselves higher? Resistance to differences reduces openness and genuine curiosity about others, their experiences, and realities, and it creates more orange barrels and narrows our path to possibilities.

As I deepen into my practices of self-reflection and connecting with my *Self*, I am more conscious than ever about how I choose to show up with others. While at lunch with a close-knit group, the energy became hostile when the topic changed to politics. I'm not fond of this topic because it depletes my energy and causes unnecessary stress. I prefer to avoid those conversations because I find them unproductive when strong opinions are shared without curiosity about alternative viewpoints. What's the point of simply stating beliefs without learning about other perspectives?

Anyway, someone sitting next to me pointed out an oversized rhinestone pin on her sweater, which was the first letter of the then-sitting U.S. President's surname. This woman was trying to provoke me, knowing our preferences differed. Good for her for asking me why I held my beliefs, but she likely was unprepared for my response. "Would you really like to know?" I asked. She said she would, but when I began to express my thoughts, she interrupted immediately with her political talking points. I stopped the conversation at that moment with, "I don't think you're really interested," and thought to myself, *isn't that interesting?* In the past, I may have participated in a debate. There was no point in continuing the discussion, and I'm glad I had enough self-awareness to set a boundary that prevented a taxing interaction. It could have been an opportunity to learn from each other, and she even remarked that I wasn't like the "others" since others were not interested in her viewpoint. Interestingly, her mind was closed as well.

If I were uncomfortable with myself, my values, and my self-beliefs, I would have shown up differently: more resistant, judgmental, potentially frustrated, or even angry. But such responses and reactions don't align with what's important to me or my life's purpose. I think I may have had a positive impact on this person, and I know I felt better about leaving the table than if we had had a heated debate. There was nothing to prove, and I didn't have to be right about anything. The freedom of not needing to be right is liberating. My lunchmates were very important people in my life, and we have stayed connected and continue to be our unique selves with our individual perspectives, values, beliefs, and purposes.

Magic can happen when we can explore, discover, and be uncomfortable, vulnerable, and open with ourselves and others. This is how we all can continue to develop the rock I refer to as your sense of self. I am a work in progress. So are you and everyone around you, even those who seem to have their act together. Millions of humans co-exist, and everyone deserves to bring their important perspective and individual talents to life.

The book called *Traction—Get a Grip on Your Business* presents a set of tools called the Entrepreneurial Operating System (EOS®), intended to help small businesses to progress toward the next level of growth. In the book, the author refers to something called Unique Ability®, which is authored and created by Catherine Nomura, Julia Waller, and Shannon Waller. He describes it as exercising a combination of your innate passions and talents in a way that surfaces your brilliance, enjoyment, and energy without consciousness.[16] Like me, this author believes every person has individual gifts waiting to be uncovered and shares,

> "When you're operating from within your Unique Ability®, your superior skill is often noticed by others who value it. You experience never-ending improvement, feel energized rather than drained, and most of all, you have a passion for what you're doing that presses you to go further…"[17]

Deepak Chopra and Eckhart Tolle have a spiritual approach to these concepts, and Gallup has a more scientific one, but I love that a business book is talking about recognizing the uniqueness of every individual as a strategy for the success of their business. Your primary strategy to achieve success is awakening yourself to your uniqueness and discovering how to bring it to life. With this, everything else will fall into place. On the way, though, one cannot take themselves too seriously.

Don't Take Yourself Too Seriously

Not taking yourself too seriously is harder than it sounds. If we're focusing mostly on outcomes and acting from a place of scarcity, it's almost impossible to enjoy the moments that make up the journey. I have learned a few tricks along the way through choice and coaching. In my twenties, I worked for a direct marketing company, which means I went door to door and business to business uninvited, with "no solicitation" signs visibly posted at the front door, to sell products and services for companies like AT&T. Upon entering each business, I greeted the receptionist and asked for the manager or owner, and when they agreed to see me, I had ten seconds to make an impression that got their attention enough for them to listen to my sales pitch.

Upon entering one business, I did not see the one-inch lip on the floor of the threshold. While walking in, I tripped and, in slow motion and without grace, ended up on my stomach in front of two gentlemen standing there, watching me. Can you imagine? Quickly picking myself up, I said something like, "What an entrance!" I laughed at myself, and the two gentlemen joined in. I got their attention and made that sale! If I hadn't created that spectacle, I may not have made the sale, so I leveraged it to my advantage.

Try This

Explore and experiment with the following ideas:

- Finding the humor in a situation
- Saying, "Isn't that interesting?" when someone states something you might otherwise take personally or become offended
- Saying the words, "Oh well" when something doesn't go your way

When something you said or did embarrasses you, try finding the humor or amusement in the situation and have yourself a good chuckle. You might as well. This is a better and healthier alternative to internalizing the situation and letting it drain your energy and confidence. Also, it will be a great share with your friends or family when they need a pick-me-up.

Another approach to undesirable moments in your life includes a couple of self-talk prompts. My life coach once shared the statement, "Isn't that interesting?" When I remember, I say this statement to myself when someone says words I perceive as rude or offensive. Sometimes, I'm able to resist the temptation to react in a way that feels disempowering. This statement takes the pressure off and helps take the personal out of the situation, encouraging a more neutral reaction.

With this technique, we're simply observing the situation instead of making it about us.

The last statement I recently discovered is, "Oh well." When something doesn't go my way and I am on the verge of reaction and emotions, sometimes this short phrase helps neutralize the situation so I can minimize my personal orange barrels and continue forward with less baggage, more energy, and a stronger *Self*.

It's Bigger Than You

Your path to building a deeper relationship with yourself is bigger than you are. This may or may not concern you, but I want you to know that something extraordinary happens when you continue to learn more about yourself, appreciate your uniqueness, have more self-compassion, and exercise less self-judgment. You are unknowingly creating space for others to do the same as you reveal limitless possibilities and feel more fulfilled, at peace, accomplished, or whatever it is you are looking for. The more welcoming and less judgmental we are of ourselves, the more welcoming and less judgmental we are of others.

Deepak Chopra points out in *The Seven Spiritual Laws of Success*, that

> "... your future is generated by the choices you are making in every moment of your life. The more you bring your choices into the level of conscious awareness, the more you will make those choices which are spontaneously correct– both for you and those around you".[18]

So, an unexpected result is your positive effect on those around you while you do the work to embrace your unfinished life and position yourself on a fruitful journey with minimal orange barrels and wider lanes. This world needs more empathy, love, compassion, curiosity, and less divisiveness. Your sense of self matters for your benefit and for the benefit of the human population. Our individual choices each day have a ripple effect on the world. Of course, when our choices are not as they should be, the effect is less than desirable. Knowing that building a stronger relationship with my *Self* affects the world around me makes me want to be more self-aware. Eckhart Tolle's quote "You are not *in* the universe, you *are* the universe"[19] is profound. You are *that* important. Being a vital piece of the universe means we participate in shaping our world, culture, and environment, whether at work, home, or in the community. To shape our world, we need to shape ourselves.

Power of the Mind

When I meditate, thoughts stream in and out of my brain. They are thoughts about the day before, and I question myself, or about the day ahead and what I need to accomplish. Random thoughts come in and out about conversations, people, my to-do list, and more. Many of these thoughts are unhelpful and may become distractions. Meditation helps me focus my mind even if only for fifteen minutes. Such random thoughts occur all day without you even thinking about them. I call this mind clutter. Mind clutter takes up space and may create orange barrels that limit our growth. While meditating one morning with Deepak Chopra, he suggested this centering thought: "My mind is my intimate friend and healer."[20] If you carried this thought through your day, how would you show up differently? Would you be kinder to yourself or judge yourself less? Would you have more self-compassion? What would happen to that negative self-talk if you view your mind as an intimate friend and healer? With less self-judgment and more self-kindness and self-compassion, what would you imagine the ripple effect would be on those around you?

The Get Organized (GO) System is a model for being organized and was something I taught to others early in my career to help them with increased productivity and personal effectiveness. One thing the model taught me was that we can only do one thing at a time effectively. When I see on job descriptions an expectation for multi-tasking, I cringe because multi-tasking is physically impossible, and it's an unrealistic expectation. We may switch our focus quickly by stopping efforts on one task and then shifting to another, but we cannot do them both well at the same time.

You might think you can multi-task well but let me ask you a couple of questions. While in a conversation with someone, you receive and answer a text. How well were you listening to the person speaking to you when you answered that text? In fact, research shows that "multitasking may seem efficient on the surface but may actually take more time in the end and involve more error" and that "even brief mental blocks created by shifting between tasks can cost as much as 40 percent of someone's productive time."[21] Let's say you are in a team meeting, class, or at a conference. While sitting there listening to the presenter, your mind wanders and thinks about the party you will go to, an argument you just had with your partner, an upcoming vacation, or something you forgot to do. What information did you miss in those few moments or seconds? You are driving and talking to someone on the phone. How many turns have you missed in this situation? I have missed so many that I can't even count them.

It's the same when we're working to build and sustain our sense of self. Unhelpful self-talk derived from past thoughts, feelings, reactions, or worries about the future is clutter and distractions to our present. How can we effectively give attention to our sense of self with so many distractions? While reading Tosha Silver's book, *Outrageous Openness*, she shared a concept she called the God Box, which is a practice designed to free us from mental clutter and make room for possibility.[22] I refer to mine as an Energy Bowl. The bowl part of the Energy Bowl is an asymmetrical bowl carved out of wood. This was a gift from a long-time friend from South Africa. When she visits her family, she often brings me a small gift, and once upon her arrival back to the states, I received this beautiful bowl.

My Energy Bowl is a way for me to write on a little piece of paper a distraction or orange barrel that is on my mind. I fold it up and give it to the universe to take care of for me. Interviewing for a job is stressful, and when I leave an interview, I try my best to say to myself, "I did my best" and then trust that whatever happens is what is supposed to happen. But this is hard to do, and I have found myself in a scarcity mindset. *Did I do enough to prepare? How long will it be before my next paycheck? Will there be other opportunities? How will I know it is the right opportunity? Can I turn it down if it's not?*

My solution was to experiment with the Energy Bowl. Tosha Silver's instructions in *Outrageous Openness* are to offer the problem to God, the divine, or the energy out there. Whatever works for you. Then forget about it.[23] So, I tried it. I wrote on a piece of paper: I know you have my back, and the right job opportunity is just within reach. That afternoon, I received a note from a recruiter about an opportunity. Each time I have offered a problem as a solution to my Energy Bowl and let it go, I have received a communication or sign that brings me a step closer to the problem being solved. Removing the thoughts and concerns from your head makes space for something else to come your way. This is an example of how your mind becomes your intimate friend. Relieve it of clutter (unwanted and unhelpful activity) so you can tap into possibilities. Tosha Silver offers a change-me prayer in her book, *It's Not Your Money*. A line in the prayer says, "Let me breathe, relax, and let you lead."[24] I love that statement. The "you" might refer to God, the universe, quantum energy, the spiritual you, or your intuition if you tap into it. You need to build a relationship with yourself and do it consciously. If you're not intentional about this, chatter, thoughts, and feelings will continue, and you will remain closed and resistant to possibilities. Let your mind be your most intimate friend and supporter.

Try This

To eliminate distracting mind clutter that impedes you, try the God Box idea. Put your own spin on it. Call it what you like. Find a box, a bowl, a vase, or anything you want to hold small folded pieces of paper. Use the following prompts to get you started:

- What is the mind clutter you are experiencing right now? What thoughts are worrying you or distracting you from important work, activities, goals, or possibilities?

    _____

    _____

- Write a question or statement that helps position the distracting thought as a solution. Fold it and drop it in your vessel of choice. Now, just let it go. It's not gone, and you won't forget it. But it is out your mind and out *there* in a place bigger than you are.

The Ripple Effect

Margaret J. Wheatley wrote a book called *Who Do We Choose to Be?* She explains that based on her experiences, there are "extraordinary leaders who were creating islands of sanity where good work still got done and where people enjoyed healthy relationships in the midst of chaotic conditions, fierce opposition, heart-breaking defeats. . ."²⁵ Wheatley mentions that in her work with leaders, she challenges them with a couple of questions, including, "Who do you choose to be?" She then turns to the reader and asks the same question. I think it is a significant question for you to consider. Your choices each day have an impact that reaches beyond you and your immediate circle. Remember that your rock is your sense of self in times of uncertainty not only for you but for others too. Like your personal ripple effect.

Imagine you are a rock that is being skipped into the water. Can you envision the ripple or rings that extend out from where the rock touches the water before sinking? This is a great metaphor for your infinite impact on the world around you. How you show up not only positions you for personal success, but also influences those in the ring nearest to where the rock hit the water. Those in that first ring influence those in the next. The goal is not to put pressure on you for fixing the world's problems, but simply to know that when we are in touch with ourselves, a better world is possible.

Summary

- *Recognize even the smallest actions and steps you have taken* to strengthen your sense of self. Then celebrate, do a little dance, or jump up and down.
- *Give yourself the gift of self-affirmation, self-reflection, and self-acceptance. You* are worthy, and your ability to enhance and maintain your sense of self depends on it.
- *Find your motivation* and knowingly sit in the awkwardness, uneasiness, and discomfort to knock down resistance and fear. There is no time like now.
- *Create a personal mission statement* to drive and align your thoughts, behaviors, and actions, as well as how

you show up in the moments, days, weeks, months, and years ahead.
- *The key to success and fulfillment is awakening to your uniqueness* and discovering how to bring these aspects of yourself to life. Everything else will fall into place. And remember not to take yourself too seriously.
- *You have an unknowing effect on others,* and your path to building a deeper relationship with yourself is bigger than you are. What you do for your *Self* has a ripple effect on others.
- Consider starting your day with the centering thought: *My mind is my intimate friend and supporter.* How will you think, feel, or behave differently with this shift in mindset?
- *Make room for new solutions and possibilities by removing unhelpful mind clutter.* Try writing your thoughts as a question or phrase on a piece of paper and asking God or the Universe for help.

PART THREE
Unearth Your Superpowers

CHAPTER EIGHT

The Superpower Principle

> There is nothing outside of yourself that can ever enable
> you to get better, stronger, richer, quicker, or smarter.
> Everything is within. Everything exists.
> See nothing outside of yourself.
>
> —Miyamoto Musashi

Superpowers. You have them. Everyone does. There are as many unique superpowers as there are people. Do you know yours? Do you know how to leverage them? This chapter is about how understanding the Superpower Principle can help you live your true and best life.

Moving on from one thing to the next involves separation, transition, and eventually, building new attachments. The excitement of moving into a bigger house in a new neighborhood can coexist with melancholy from leaving behind neighbors, teachers, and familiar faces at local establishments for example. Sometimes leaving a company was my choice, and other times, it was not. Each time, I noticed a winding-down process as my last day approached. Suddenly, out of the woodwork came compliments, affirmation, words of appreciation, and even unexpected hugs from people. I learned new things about what people most admired about me as a colleague. One of my favorites was when someone referred to me as *refreshing*, and I began to reflect on what that meant and how I had this quality others noticed before I did. It turns out that being *refreshing* is one of my superpowers. Sometimes traits that make us feel as if we don't fit in are our superpowers, and when we claim and unleash them, we flourish because we're being authentic.

Superpowers Defined

Let's break down the idea of superpowers using Marvel movies, such as *Spider-Man, The Avengers,* and *Black Panther*, all based on a well-known series of comic books written by Stan Lee. These movie series are all about the battle between good and evil. The movies bring the comic book characters to life, and the superhero characters carry the burden of fighting with and overcoming the evil forces so the world can shine and be her best self. Marvel movies are exciting and entertaining to watch, and I also think they are relevant because they reflect the conflict and disharmony in the real world and in our inner worlds.

Of all the Marvel movies, *Iron Man* is at the top of my list, partly because Robert Downey Jr. plays the main character.[26] When he is not in superhero mode, he is Tony Stark, who owns Stark Industries, a manufacturer of weapons founded by his father. Tony is flawed, but he also has a gift—his genius IQ. He's an inventor who designs the most innovative weapons of mass destruction sold to the U.S. government. Also, he's arrogant, lacks compassion for others, and thinks only about himself. His self-awareness about the dark side of his genius is nonexistent. His arrogance prevents him from being open to being challenged, and he is resistant to gaining insight into the world outside of himself and his business.

And then comes the inciting action that prompts his transformation. Tony makes a trip to Afghanistan, where Stark Industries sells weapons. He gets kidnapped by terrorists who are using his weapons to murder innocent civilians and discovers how his company has been complicit in the corruption and destruction. During this time of turmoil, Tony discovers his core values and is on a new mission. He stops the mass production of weapons and shifts his focus to building a single weapon—an Iron Man suit, designed to save people and destroy the corrupt system that allows mass murder. His goal is to destroy weapons of mass destruction.

At first, the Iron Man suit appears to give Tony Stark superpowers, but his self-awareness and growing connection with himself empower him. His new sense of self is his most transforming superpower. He has clarity about how he wants to show up in the world now. Still, he's not perfect and remains arrogant. But Tony has shifted his view of himself in the world, which will drive his future decisions and actions. His intent is pure, and he makes mistakes—lots of them. Tony falls into old behaviors as people and events continue to challenge him, but he has awakened and continues to reflect, learn, and become more aware of who he is and what is important to him.

If we break down the word superpower, consider power to be the gasoline or electricity that fuels a car, for example, to move from point A to point B. This substance becomes a catalyst for acceleration or momentum to get somewhere and accomplish something. If you run out of fuel, you lose momentum. Like Tony Stark in the *Iron Man* movie, your personal fuel is a clear sense of *Self*. Power is also about influence and effect. Remember the ripple effect we talked about earlier? Each one of us influences others, regardless if we are aware of it, in either large deliberate ways or minute unintentional ones. We influence how others feel about themselves and behave, and the actions they take based on what we think of ourselves, how we behave, and what we model.

The other part of the word superpower is *super*. Super means intensified. Your best self is *You* intensified. Often, others appreciate your gifts even if no one says it. Even if you are not meeting expectations, your superpowers are there, waiting to be expressed. If you are not in an environment that appreciates your true *Self*, it may be difficult to be aware of what your best self looks like. When you are your true and best self, you are aware of your superpowers because they shine. You shine. Things feel easier, and you are in the flow. You feel more fulfilled and energized and look forward to starting your day, whether you head to work, school, or a day with your children or friends. Also, you don't need others' approval, but when you get it, it's only a confirmation of what you already know.

No Checking the Box

My husband and I started a tradition to celebrate our anniversary. We take time to share ten things we appreciate about each other. Because my husband knows my primary language of love is words of affirmation, he graciously agrees to do this exercise every year. It has turned out to be easy for us to name things, and that energy stays with me for the next few days. As I have grown in self-awareness, I have been able to ask for what I need, such as occasional words of affirmation. I end up feeling valued and appreciated, and my husband feels good, too, meeting one of my needs.

Practicing the techniques in this book has helped in narrowing my sense-of-self gap on the continuum. I'm working on not needing others to validate my worth. It's a long-term project, but I'm making progress. The more I get to know myself, my talents and strengths, and create the space to be myself, the less affirmation I need from others. I now know I have superpowers unique to me. Some days, they are top of mind, and other days I forget they're there. When I can't share them freely, it may be because I am not open to them, and I have to determine whether I am depleting or energizing myself. When I feel I can be my genuine *Self*, my superpowers naturally get to work. Your genuine *Self* is your superpower.

This book has been focusing on building the foundation you need to unleash your superpowers. Without embracing the process of discovery to connect with yourself, the Superpower Principle cannot fully come to life. No checking the box here. Your life deserves more than checking items off a to-do list. How you approach strengthening the relationship with your *Self* determines how many orange barrels or single lanes might impede living a fulfilling life. Realizing and expressing your superpowers requires a deeper commitment from you and is more complex than going to the grocery store, finishing the laundry, or continuing to do what you do because it's what you've already done. Stepping up and trying new things is an important part of your lifelong evolution toward your best self.

Accepting the status quo or going through the motions describes complacency. Throughout my working years, I have seen and experienced a lot of status quo and interacted with many employees who seemed only to be going through the motions, just checking boxes. For someone who is consciously purposeful, this environment is not ideal. Not long after I began a new role at an organization, I mentioned an idea while walking with my colleague to a meeting. His response was, "That's not the way we do it around here." How many times have you heard this statement? There's nothing worse as a new employee than hearing your ideas are not welcome. I give my colleague credit because when I responded with, "I thought you hired me because of the value I can bring from my experiences," he responded with, "You're right. We did," and then followed up with an apology. I give myself credit, too, for responding authentically to his statement.

Contributing to the better is part of my personal mission. I feel a sense of responsibility to contribute to making things better because it's good for everyone, including me and my family. But this always begins with a truer *Me*. Knowing what it means to be true influences how I contribute to and engage with the world and whether I unleash my superpowers. My commitment to contributing to the *better* affects others, beginning with those close to me, and then fanning out to others, just like the ripples from that rock tossed into the lake.

Swimming Downstream

Decades of self-talk, getting clearer and more confident about my sense of self, and overcoming a multitude of self-inflicted orange barrels got me to where I am today. It took me a long time to get here. Time will tell, but I think I have found my place and my people at a company whose purpose is to make the world a better place. They bring out the best in people, starting with their own employees. I would not be here without reflecting, getting to know *Me* and what I value at a deeper level, and consciously reducing my level of resistance to what comes my way. I'm still not done though. But instead of feeling discouraged, I feel liberated by the possibilities for further growth. As I am maturing in life emotionally and physically, I know I have more than ever to contribute. I'm in my mid-fifties now, and my desire to contribute extends beyond work. I'm going for limitless, which we cannot yet define!

If you feel blocked from achieving and living your true and best self, there are plenty of suggested experiments inside and outside of this book. Your superpowers cannot shine through with the intensity you deserve if you feel stuck. There's no time like the present to try things that might shift your mind in small but powerful ways. Even a minor mindset shift creates new thoughts, feelings, and behaviors that will stay with you on the path to your next best Self.

Ken Blanchard is a business consultant, motivational speaker, one of the top twenty-five best-selling authors of all time, and co-founder of The Ken Blanchard Companies. He developed a program called Situational Leadership. Situational Leadership is one of my favorite leadership development programs and one of the most effective theories for developing people and bringing out their best. The program empowers leaders to provide the right amount of support and direction necessary to each individual team member on each task or goal they must achieve. What I love about the Situational Leadership philosophy is that it steers leaders away from broad-brushing one style of leading and developing their teams. The core of Situational Leadership is the belief that each of us has various levels of competence and confidence related to each task or goal we must achieve. Our level of experience with that task or goal determines our level of competence and confidence. A major tenet of the program is that everyone wants and deserves to develop. Part of the curriculum includes a discussion about this principle because research also shows that not all leaders believe it.

In fact, each time I have facilitated this leadership development session, some participants have disagreed with the tenet. They have stated that lazy and underperforming employees don't want to develop or that retiring professionals don't want to focus on it. Maybe you agree. However, if you think about development as continuous growth and learning because we are living an unfinished life of possibilities, the paradigm might shift. Who wants to continue to underperform? Who wants to be perceived as lazy? Are those who are retiring done? Maybe, but I would argue that everyone wants to feel appreciated and be their best selves no matter where they are in life.

Unfinished

Have you ever felt your stars align? Did everything seem to fall into place and you could breathe easy, relax, and feel as though someone lifted a burden from your shoulders? Once the weight lifted, did you feel as if you were flowing with the current instead of against it, as if you were in the zone? In these moments, your superpowers are begging to come out to play, which means your sense of self was strong in that moment.

Last Full Measure is a movie based on a true story that brings the Superpower Principle to life.[27] The film is a great illustration of what it feels like to be in the zone. The zone can only appear when one is deeply connected with the *Self*. A young man named William Pitsenbarger (Bill) was a United States Air Force pararescueman during the Vietnam War. Pararescue teams had been in place since before World War II, and they find soldiers, provide medical attention, and retrieve the injured from combat.

The pararescue training program has been referred to as Superman School. In the movie, Bill was part of the pararescue team that flew in on helicopters to rescue injured soldiers from the trenches in the Vietnam War. The scene showed the medic and other soldiers carrying the injured to the metal body basket that attached to the helicopter. Those in the helicopter scooped up the injured, stabilized them to the best of their ability, and took them to safety for further treatment.

In one scene, the U.S. troops were under fire from all angles. In the helicopter above the trees, Bill realized someone had to descend to the ground to help the troops. No one else volunteered, so Bill took hold of the chain and, without regard for his own safety, held his head high and gave the signal to lower him to the ground. Bullets blasted all around him, but none pierced his body. It was as if he were swimming downstream in the flow and stepping up to the challenge with no fear or second-guessing, only acting. It was as if he repelled the bullets.

Troops dropped like flies, and those who didn't stared at Bill in awe. After treating multiple wounded soldiers, Bill could have gone back to the helicopter where his pararescue teammates were calling him, waving their arms, and begging him to come back. He couldn't bring himself to leave those who needed him. Bill knew himself and knew what he had to do. For him, the choice was easy; there was no choice. His actions aligned with his values and purpose, and because he was true to himself, many lives were saved. In the film, we fast forward thirty years, and Bill's father shared that when Bill enlisted in military service as a young adult, he did not ask his father's permission. He simply told his father of his plans and left one morning without an announcement to relieve his father of any guilt if something should happen to him. Bill felt called, and he answered the call.

For whatever unjust reason, the military downgraded the top honor Bill should have received for his selfless actions. Throughout the years that followed, many who served with Bill tried repeatedly to rectify the situation. The enemy had defeated those around him in combat that day. It scared the soldiers to death, and they felt hopeless when Bill swooped in, acted, and provided direction to the troops while saving life after life with ease as if he wore an Iron Man suit.

Eventually, the military recognized Bill's heroism. Officials, his parents, fellow pararescuers, soldiers, and others finally gathered to present the highest honor for Bill's actions thirty years earlier. At the end of the ceremony, the key official and presenter went off script to ask those present to stand up if Bill's actions that day in combat directly affected them. Along with Bill's parents, those Bill had saved rose from their seats, followed by their family members, their children, and their children's children. Over one hundred people were present and Bill had touched each of them, even if they had never met him.

Sharing this story is not about Bill finally getting the recognition he deserved, although I felt joy knowing that. The movie is an example of the power of the sense of self as our rock and the unimaginable and unknowing ripple effect it has on others. When we connect with ourselves and can be our true selves, regardless of whether we are aware of it, our superpowers affect others. Think of Bill as a rock tossed into a lake and imagine the ripples. Bill's ripple effect radiated outward for generations. He was not aware of it, and recognition did not drive him. His motivation came from knowing his purpose and who he was from the inside out—what he valued and what was important to him. Then he aligned with that by doing what he knew he had to do.

Are you ready to embrace the Superpower Principle in your own life? Here are some key points from this chapter for review and future reference.

Summary

- *There are as many superpowers as people.* You have superpowers, regardless of whether you are aware of them. Strengthening your sense of self is the key to unleashing them.

- *The "power" in superpowers is your fuel, a clear sense of self,* which causes that ripple effect, as when you toss a stone into the water. This ripple is a source of personal power as an influence on others and its effect.

- The "super" in superpower means intensified. *Your best self is You intensified.* Others appreciate you and your gifts, and they exist, even if those around you don't verbalize them or see them.

- *When you are your true and best Self, you are aware of your superpowers* because they can be unleashed. You shine. Things feel easier, and you are "in the flow."

- *Exploring, discovering, and connecting with yourself is the catalyst* for the Superpower Principle to come to life. Trying different things is a key factor in achieving the limitless state.

CHAPTER NINE

Shifting Expectations

> We can each define ambition and progress for ourselves. The goal is to work toward a world where expectations are not set by the stereotypes that hold us back, but by our personal passion, talents and interests.
>
> —Sheryl Sandberg

This chapter is about expectations. Have societal or other people's ideas about what you should expect from yourself and others trapped you? Expectations can distract you from achieving flow and bringing your superpowers to life. When your expectations—of yourself and others—go unmet, it could cause disappointment and defeat for you and those onto whom you project the expectations, which might sabotage your happiness.

Linger in the Moments

It's tempting to gauge success by our expectations of visible and tangible outcomes alone, such as houses, cars, clothing brands, or the latest and greatest technology. But don't overlook the small but mighty moments of greatness. Each day begins with tasks that we must complete, and we all work toward achieving outcomes that provide something better and more desirable for the companies we work for and ourselves. The outcome is often the measure of success. Then we spend only a few moments on other rewards, such as a pat on the back or a few words of acknowledgment. When we focus only on the outcomes, we forget the moments of progress along the way, and the learning, growth, and feeling like we're contributing to something bigger. Those moments fuel our sense of self.

For too many of us, though, the journey between the assigned task and its completion is exhausting, overwhelming, and depleting. Instead of feeling uplifted, many feel overworked, under-resourced, and under-appreciated. Does the actual outcome compensate for all this? What if it doesn't? Are the outcomes meaningful to us? What if they're not? Do we allow the *Self* to lead us to the place we really want to go? Depending on outcomes to fill our bucket, define our sense of self, and reach self-fulfillment, pride, happiness, and engagement means relinquishing control over our lives. Allowing the *Self* to lead requires us to take responsibility for our own happiness, which sometimes means shifting expectations about our current situation or finding the courage to leave a workplace that simply cannot unleash our best.

Being your authentic *Self* makes you unstoppable. Don't stop dreaming, reaching, or setting goals. I couldn't live my day-to-day meaningfully if nothing was drawing me toward the future. But the moment-to-moment experiences are where we live, so celebrate the tiniest of successes. They keep you going.

How are you managing the tension between expectations, reality, and your responsibility to make choices that contribute to your defined success? Remember the uplifting moments and experiences along the way as you improve your capacity to self-reflect on these things. The journey takes up the most space in our lives, so if you forget about the journey, you miss out on most of your life. You might believe that life will be better when *(fill in the blank)*; or you'll be happier when *(fill in the blank)*; or you won't have any worries when *(fill in the blank)*. You miss out if you don't consider the time between today and a future state.

Try shifting your expectations to make room for more enjoyment. Sometimes, you must set an intention to do things that make you feel good. Like any habit, it will get easier to feel joy, receive kindness from others, and embrace the thousands of in-between moments and experiences along the way, even if they're not great. It all starts with defining what is important to you, then lingering in those moments when it happens and enjoying the heck out of it! Notice the moments of joy, calm, and presence. Be conscious of the space you are in, how you are feeling, what you are thinking, and how you're showing up in life on that day.

Surely, you've already discovered more about yourself at this point in the book. Maybe you sense a deeper understanding of what is important to you, or you've realized how the people who surround you are contributing to or detracting from your truest and best Self. Prioritizing your capacity to be *You* will accelerate the journey to accomplishing your dreams, goals, and desires, and loosen you up to receive those subtle moments and experiences along the way.

Shifting your expectations of yourself and others will take an emotional weight off your shoulders. Living with fewer preconceived expectations and rigid ideas about specific outcomes is a step toward aligning what is important to you with a more conscious and intentional approach to each day and moment. When too many expectations (what you think *should* be or happen) take up permanent residence in your mind, you've squeezed out room to imagine and receive possibilities you aren't aware of yet.

Being True to the Inner Sometimes Requires Resistance to the Outer

Margaret Wheatley, in her book, *Who Do We Choose to Be*, suggests that humans are living in an age of decadence and trapped by a mindset of *what's-in-it-for-me* thinking.[28] It's hard to deny this, and I wonder to what extent I have contributed and enabled that mindset. It seems true we've gone overboard in being preoccupied with our individual wants and needs. How does being true to ourselves rub up against the larger systems in which we are trying to exist? We set expectations for ourselves and others based on the external world versus our inner world. How does your intrinsic motivation square with fitting into the larger collective society? The ego facilitates us fitting into the external world and may prevent the inner authentic pieces of us from showing up. If this is the case, it will be difficult to find and sustain an authentic and meaningful definition of success.

Early in my career, my goal was to become a vice president within the human resources department. When they promoted me to director, which was an incremental step toward my all-time goal of vice president, I was so excited. But a year later, they eliminated my position. Although I wasn't the only one to suffer during the recession that began in 2008, this first-time experience provoked a pendulum-like shift in my sense of self. A myriad of feelings, such as fear, humiliation, disappointment, and anger flooded me. Oddly, I also felt relief. Unemployment plunged me into a scarcity mindset, but lots of self-talk and supportive, uplifting people helped keep me grounded and positive—most of the time.

Eight months into my job search, I interviewed for two companies simultaneously. I strongly preferred one job, and it looked as if I would get it, but before the expected offer, they put the position on hold because of a leadership change. I was so disappointed. The other company offered me a job in a similar role and even paid more, but the title was not as prestigious. Because I did not meet the expectation of the specific title that my definition of success demanded, I felt deflated, as if I had taken a step back. I accepted the offer anyway and remember the powerful blow to my ego at that moment.

Deepak Chopra describes the ego as "... your self-image, your social mask, a role you are playing. Your social mask tends to thrive on approval, it wants to control, and it is sustained by power, because it lives in fear".[29] We play lots of roles, including parent, employee, friend, and partner, and we conform our behavior and expectations to our role we are playing at the time. The ego is protective, which is good, but it also can be detrimental.

Securing that first promotion fed my ego's need for external validation. Then, when I lost that job, it crushed my ego. It was as if the validation had never happened. Taking a step back in my career frightened and embarrassed me. I had associated my identity with being a director, something extrinsic, and I felt *less than* with the new manager title. Accepting that I had to go back to the manager title was difficult. I remember mentioning to someone, "I think I just discovered I have an ego." But it was a gift because I had a new awareness of my inner world. It sounds ridiculous, but the preoccupation with my title and sense of identity cluttered my mind for two years. In hindsight, it became a barrier to happiness and joy, blocking my enjoyment of moments and experiences. I did not enjoy working for that company for several reasons, but I am certain my focus on a title as my identity was a prime contributor. Thank goodness for the colleagues and partners with whom I had a strong connection. Besides being some of the smartest, most talented people I had ever worked with, they were uplifting, prominent advocates, and good friends. They added meaning and magic to my days despite my subconscious attempts to devalue my *Self*.

Some people look back and realize they've changed their minds many times about what they wanted to do for a living. That's my daughter. First, it was a firefighter, then a veterinarian, and then CEO of a company. Not me. I knew since elementary school that I wanted to be an artist. When my daughter was a pre-teen, I asked about her thoughts for her future, and her answer was unsettling. She said something like, "It doesn't matter. Everyone hates their job anyway." Whoa! I wondered what I might be accidentally modeling for my daughter. I sure didn't want her entering her work life with that perspective. The expectation I had for myself—having a prestigious title—was limiting my possibilities and my ability to tap into my true *Self*. My purpose then had been more about a title than leading a meaningful life, and that ended up draining me. My daughter felt it even if I couldn't see it. Those words and that moment became one of the many pivotal times in my life.

Remember the concept of ripples that spread from one action? My feelings and thoughts, shaped by my protective ego, influenced how I had shown up at home, which then impacted my daughter's view of the world. Her comment hit me with the force a bowling ball has on a pin. If I hadn't realized her perspective at that moment, she may have entered her adult life with unhelpful thoughts and feelings, which would have influenced the choices she made and their effect on other people.

Not being true to myself impeded me. I went to work feeling *less than*, and I probably behaved less than. This negatively affected my confidence and how I showed up each day at work and with my family. Feeling *less than* contributed to a lower level of engagement, joy, confidence, and feeling of success. Once I saw the ripple effect of my daughter's ideas about work, I made a change. I knew the company I worked for was not a good fit for me. Also, my ego took over with disastrous effect. Eckhart Tolle said when one feels stuck in an undesirable situation, there are three choices available: accept it if you can live with it, change it if you can, or leave it.[30] I left it because I didn't want to continue feeling depleted from limiting myself. It was time to find something that matched my unfolding purpose and desire to give to others more fully.

On what do you base your sense of identity? Being a provider? Your circle of friends? Where you live or the car you drive? Peel back the layers of your social mask and see what's underneath those surface-level definitions of your worth. You might find your true *Self*. If you don't have the slightest idea about how you would answer this question, you may want to re-read some of the earlier chapters of this book. Have you limited yourself with your expectations? The director's title was my social mask and status, and I valued it. I was proud of many accomplishments at that organization and of the relationships I had cultivated. I did the best I could in my mind and, fortunately, met amazing colleagues, many with whom I still stay in touch. One of them is still my best friend. But I wasn't happy, and I didn't feel as if I were enough during my time with that company.

Eventually, I discovered the title didn't define who I was. Instead, the nature of the work, the responsibilities of the title, and whether they aligned with how I operated when I was at my best all contributed to what I thought and knew about myself. I'm in flow when I can share a vision and build a strategy to achieve it, influence and meaningfully bring people on a journey, and elevate the employee experience. When I am at my best at work, it is because the company allows me to leverage my talents and be true to myself while I do work that aligns with my core being and values. I have had experiences

Shifting Expectations

where this is the case and others where it is not. That scenario makes a difference in how I feel about going to work every day, how I feel about myself doing the work, and the gap in my sense-of-self continuum.

By now you know I am a fan of Deepak Chopra and Eckhart Tolle. They have been helping me on my journey to being and living as my true self. Deepak Chopra's seventh spiritual law of success, from his book *The Seven Spiritual Laws of Success,* is the Law of Dharma, which is essentially about being aware of your unique talents, expressing them in your unique way, and using them to help others.[31] This is another way of practicing the Superpower Principle. The Law of Dharma brings your superpowers to life, embracing them as the gifts they are, and acting on them as your life's purpose. I am not a religious person, but I didn't recognize that I was a spiritual person until my fifties, with the help of others. Prior to that, I confused religion with spirituality.

According to Chopra, "Our true Self is spiritual, that essentially, we are spiritual beings that have taken manifestation in physical form".[32] Knowing your *Self* is vital to feeling clarity during uncertain times. You may have discovered that when you do something with passion and genuine engagement, time flies or you are in flow, which is how some describe the state of being fully present. "When you are expressing that one unique talent that you possess—or more than one unique talent in many cases—the expression of that talent takes you into timeless awareness."[33] This is the second component of the Law of Dharma. The third and last component is using those gifts to serve others. This one falls into place naturally and takes on the infinite ripple effect.

Try This

Revisit your personal mission statement from Chapter Seven. Don't worry if it's messy or imperfect. Think about whether you have tapped into and leveraged the true *You*. Give a little thought to the following questions.

- What are your genuine gifts and talents? What uplifts you and brings you energy? If you are finding it difficult to realize your gifts and talents, think about something you accomplished in the past weeks or months that felt easy, brought you genuine joy, or in which you felt pride. (For example, you solved a problem for a customer that made them feel important, finished writing a script, found a new love and energy in creating a podcast episode, baked a cake or enjoyed cooking a new dish, sold a home, or threw your child a birthday party that made them smile from ear to ear.)

  _____
  _____
  _____

- If you're struggling to appreciate something about yourself, what's interfering?

  _____
  _____
  _____

- How are you limiting yourself? What expectations do you have of yourself that are too specific and limit the possibilities?

  _____
  _____
  _____

- Have you aligned your expectations with your values, purpose, and what's important to you?

  _____
  _____
  _____

- How have your expectations of yourself detracted from your real purpose? How do you need to shift them?

  _____
  _____
  _____

AND Thinking

Like the other activities suggested in this book, there are no right or wrong answers. The goal here is simply reflection and taking stock of how you are intentionally aligning with your true and best self each moment of each day. When you think about it, you may discover that you have rigid or narrow expectations of yourself. I have them, and I have a way of thinking about this called AND thinking. You may have some limiting expectations AND at the same time you can build a deeper relationship with your *Self*. Life is not black and white or one *or* the other—it can be one *and* the other. It is messy and full of gray, and that's okay. We are a work in progress.

Deepak Chopra's first spiritual law of success is Pure Potentiality. "The field of pure potentiality is your own Self. And the more you experience your true nature, the closer you are to the field of pure potentiality."[34] Your true nature comes to life when you loosen up your preconceived notions or expectations of what life should be and connect more deeply with your Self, your talents, and what naturally motivates and drives you. Shift your expectations by putting less emphasis on the extrinsic and material and more emphasis on the intrinsic motivations hiding out in your inner world.

You deserve to participate in your life journey by aligning with what is important to you. You can still aim for your extrinsic goals *AND*, at the same time, increase your intentions of bringing your deeper values and *Self* to life. The *AND* thinking represents hope and can healthily alter your assumptions and approach. It reminds us that progress matters, and our progress is the fuel that keeps us energized, engaged, and fulfilled. The *AND* thinking can help us feel ready to go, settled, and uplifted instead of exhausted, anxious, and disappointed because it opens us to possibilities. If you feel depleted, you are neither tapping into your deeper self nor exercising AND thinking.

Throughout this book, I have emphasized focusing on building a stronger relationship and connecting more deeply with your *Self*. I have also shared that we focus too much on the self in this world. This might sound like a contradiction, so let me clarify. The collective focus on what benefits *me* as a member of society combined with a lack of curiosity about and empathy for others has erected an imaginary and stubborn wall that intensifies our us-versus-them society. Just listen to the news or conversations around you. The artificial division that many succumb to benefits those who have more, enlarging the gap between the haves and have-nots.

Margaret Wheatly's book *Who Do We Choose to Be?* mentions the Shambhala people. They are from the mythical kingdom of Shambala, which means the source of happiness, and various ancient texts have been written about it. Shambala people see the threats to humans and our Earth and step up, "armed with only two weapons: compassion and insight."[35] The focus on self that is troublesome in our world is based on desires for external things, including material possessions, status, and power. The Shambhala people see how

Shifting Expectations

such desires have impeded the human spirit and threatened the continuity of our Earth and environment.

Wheatley describes herself as a "Warrior for the Human Spirit."[36] She doesn't derive her sense of self from material acquisitions but from personal values, core beliefs, and a deeper relationship with her inner self. Connecting with your inner self manifests as embracing natural gifts that contribute to the infinite ripple when we express them. Your purpose need not affect the entire world. That is a lot to worry about. My point is that being *You* is better for you and everyone else without you even thinking about it. Being better, kinder, more compassionate, patient, and honoring and aligning with what's important to you will *naturally* result in you doing the same for others.

Parents, teachers, and mentors have taught us to set and even stretch goals and to outperform others instead of simply being our best. We are competitive, and often the goal is to win by ranking yourself above others. Our physical surroundings can nourish or simply enhance the needs of our ego. The size of our home, the car we drive, the clothes we wear, and the title we wear at work may all fortify the ego. There is nothing wrong with driving nice cars, living in a lovely home, or making a substantial income. I like those things too. They make us feel momentarily better about ourselves and our situation and give us a sense of security, but they may also contribute to a false sense of self.

You can tell how attached you are to the ways of the ego by imagining how you would feel if you lost those items tomorrow. These nice-to-have possessions may prevent us from feeling fulfilled. In our minds, we set expectations for what life is supposed to be like, and when we don't achieve our vision, we feel disappointed. Changing our expectations can liberate us, and now I strive to start my days by intending to embrace and celebrate what comes my way instead of clinging to some idea of how the day should go. Will you join me?

The Magic of Beginners Luck

My friend told me a story about an adventure she and her husband experienced before marriage. One night in college, they tried off-track, horse race betting. They had never done this before and did not know what to expect. They arrived with one-hundred dollars and chose three horses betting on the first-, second-, and third-place winners. If the three horses they chose crossed the finish line first in the order they chose, this is called a trifecta. What are the chances of identifying the first-, second-, and third-place winners concurrently, especially given that they had no experience or knowledge of this sport? They left the off-track facility as winners of nearly two-thousand dollars as seniors in college.

This took place thirty years ago, and the win felt like a ton of money for a couple of college kids. Have you heard the phrase beginner's luck? Have you experienced it? Do you really understand what beginner's luck is? It's about assuming nothing big will happen, having zero expectations. And then you relish in the pure energy of trying something without the need to expect an outcome. It's fun, and there's no pressure. With openness and no preconceived notions, possibilities increase exponentially. Beginner's luck experiences are great examples of being aware and embracing the present situation. Just think about the possibilities if we could limit our expectations and only be in the moment more often.

What are you trying to improve, enhance, or learn right now? Do you have a weight loss goal, or are you trying to incorporate more exercise and meditation into your day? Are you trying to be happier, stop procrastinating, achieve a better life balance, take up blogging, read more, or write a book? The desires are limitless, but so are the possibilities. Most of us have something we're working on, trying to learn, dedicating more time to, or improving. In my field of talent development, there are so many goals I know are achievable.

They're just too massive, too broad, not realistic or measurable, and do not set up employees for success.

When I was trying to get into the best shape of my life before age forty, my nutritionist taught me to design flexible expectations that would align with what was important to me. For instance, I enjoyed wine and lattes and chose not to remove these delights from my diet. She asked me questions and presented options I could wrap my head around and not feel like a failure. I didn't realize focusing on days of exercise versus hours of exercise could make a difference. There are multiple approaches for each goal, and each of us needs to find the one that aligns with what we can commit to. Committing to doing something every day is too narrow for me. Have you thought about how to adapt strategies to increase the likelihood of your success?

Shifting expectations is not the same as being lazy. Find your pace, level of commitment, and what works for you. If you try something and it doesn't work, try something else. Break it down into smaller pieces. Don't give up. Don't give up on *You*. You've got this. Do something. Act, no matter how small. Be proud and choose to recognize, be aware of, and celebrate small moments of progress. In an earlier chapter, I shared an example of one type of tracking system I used for myself and taped onto the refrigerator for daily visibility. It was quite unsophisticated, and there were weeks when I didn't achieve what I wanted. *Tomorrow is another day*, I told myself. I am comforted by my commitment to a lifelong journey of connecting with and building a better relationship with myself every day, whether it's through exercise, meditation, writing, journaling, or some days, nothing at all.

The following summary includes quick reminders of the key points included in this chapter.

Summary

- *Take a load off your shoulders by shifting your expectations.* When your mind is full of what you think you should do and what should happen, you won't have room for the possibilities that you haven't yet imagined. The less cluttered and more open your mind, the more room there is for you to receive and achieve.

- *There are millions of moments on the journey* to achievement that make up most of your life. Be aware of more of them, then celebrate and share them. Don't depend only on periodic and monumental outcomes and results to fuel and energize You.

- *You deserve to participate in a life journey that aligns with what is important to you.* You can still aim for extrinsic goals *AND* increase your intention to bring your deeper values and *Self* to life.

- *Being better, kinder, more compassionate,* patient, and honoring and aligning with what's important to you will *naturally* result in you doing the same for others. How cool is that?

CHAPTER TEN

Small but Mighty

> My life has changed because of the constant application of small changes over a long period of time.
>
> —Anonymous

Do your days always begin with a mile-long list of tasks to accomplish? It feels great to check those boxes, to prove to someone else or us that we have achieved something. But the list never seems to end, does it? Will there ever be an ultimate feeling of achievement or closure? Emails, projects, homework, and cleaning never feel finished. The weeds keep growing in the garden, and it seems the grass was just cut yesterday, but now it needs cutting again. I'm an artist, so bear with me for a moment while I use a metaphor from an artist's point of view. Think of your life as a gallery or museum full of artifacts and masterpieces that you have collected along your life's journey. Not physical or literal artifacts but moments of achievement and accomplishments that make you proud. If you have ever walked through a gallery or museum, you might not have noticed that they include seating areas for reflection to honor individual and collective masterpieces, inventions, people, and history.

The creators of those pieces likely never imagined their projects and passions would be part of a historical collection for us to honor, admire, learn from, and view for eternity. That probably wasn't their goal either. The collections make it possible to appreciate the millions of moments in an unfinished and ever-developing journey of exceptional people, many of whom did not reap the financial benefits of their work. They created because they had a calling that aligned with their natural talents and sense of purpose. I imagine each of these artists surrendered to a deeper part of themselves, embraced their uniqueness, trusted the process, and continuously grew in their self-awareness and sense of self.

I call these moments in time *small but mighty*. They don't feel that important individually, but the collection of these moments drives progress. Without the smaller and individual moments, getting to the better and the next is impossible. We should acknowledge, honor, reflect upon, and leverage our ongoing and small but mighty experiences along the way for inspiration. We can easily overlook these everyday experiences, but without them, not one of us would achieve the last piece or outcome that becomes part of our personal and metaphorical museum or gallery.

Try This

What small but mighty moments have you neglected to acknowledge or celebrate? Take a few moments to think about one or more small but mighty experiences within the past week that deserve attention. Not the big result or outcome, but one of the everyday moments. Maybe you received an affirmation from someone, set an intention, successfully ate smaller portions, or skipped dessert. You might have avoided procrastination and started a task, got to that book chapter, or made yourself journal a couple of lines. Perhaps you realized you were present enough to enjoy a sunset, reflected on how you responded to a triggering event, successfully pushed away an undesirable thought, or cleaned out the junk drawer. Maybe you just took a few moments to breathe deeply.

- In the space below, reflect on a small but mighty moment. Bring it to life, tell a story, honor it, and consider how your reflection is contributing to your growth and outlook for the future.

_____
_____
_____

What emotions did you feel during this exercise? Did you feel good, or was it uncomfortable? For some of you, it's difficult to appreciate yourself because you think it's bragging. Be aware of your emotions and reflect on those too. Are you proud of yourself for taking the action? Did you have to muster some courage? Do you want to celebrate? Do it! Are you feeling progress now in your unfinished life? I'm feeling it for you.

Waking up to Yourself

Being your authentic self can be challenging because we live our lives as small, collective groups of people. To achieve certain career goals, for example, we must adapt to our company's culture. To be flexible and work on a team could energize or deplete us, depending on whether the culture is a good match. Without a strong sense of self, we may stay in a toxic situation for too long. Life feels hard sometimes, and we may need to exercise small but mighty boosts of courage to show up authentically, which might feel risky.

You never know when a small but mighty opportunity might show up. As my sisters and I were approaching forty, we began celebrating each of our milestone birthdays in Mexico. We loved staying in less commercialized areas that offered more authentic experiences. We always stayed in small hotels on the beach and sought cozy places that would give us a taste of local culture. On one trip, we pulled ourselves away from the beach and took a day trip to a huge natural water park. The ocean currents fed the lazy river through an inlet. You could not possibly be lazy to get back to where you started.

We were enjoying the fast flow of our bodies through the mangroves in the warm salt water, soaking up the sun. And then our attention quickly turned upward to the long line of people waiting to jump off a cliff that was about four to five meters high. My sister proclaimed she had nothing to prove, and I agreed. *Too scary*, I thought. But something that I couldn't shake made me want to try it. It was one of those moments, and I knew I'd regret not trying. I hopped off the tube, found the path to the top of the cliff, and lined up with the other adventurers.

When it was my turn to take that leap, I ran to the edge and stopped. The collective giggles felt like understanding and a gentle nudge to try again. I ran to the edge and stopped again. I was feeling awkward now holding up the line, so I let a few others hop in front of me. I had lots of self-talk as I tried to muster up some courage to jump. My sisters and strangers were shouting, "You can do it! You can do it!" And then ... I did it! I jumped. Whew! The experience was a combination of terror and exhilaration. When I found my way to the surface of the water and caught my breath, I felt proud and energized. I wanted to do it again, so I did. It was still terrifying and still took me a few tries before making it into the air and colliding with the water.

We all got back on our tubes and continued down the lazy river. I lingered in my feelings of gratitude for my courage and the adrenaline rush, then wondered what I had been afraid of. Was it a fear of getting hurt by hitting my head on a rock beneath the water? Was it the potential embarrassment of losing my swimsuit top or bottom? I didn't know for sure, but I suspect it was fear of the unknown and uncertainty of the situation that terrified me the most. Taking that risk resulted in an outstanding experience, and I recognized fears that were beneath the surface of my life.

Many of us live our lives full of fear and resistance, so maybe the fear of jumping off a cliff into the water is a useful metaphor. What are we afraid of? Not fitting in? Others not liking us? Being judged? Some of my fear comes from not knowing what will happen if I don't please certain people. What will happen? I haven't figured it all out yet. When my daughter was younger, she described many kids in her class as weird. My response was consistently, "Everyone is weird." Why should we all be the same? What fun is that? We might describe others based on our own perception of what is ordinary, but who wants to be ordinary? Ordinary is numbing, confining, and hinders our ability to be our authentic and best self. Being like everyone else and playing a role that is not the genuine *You* are draining and depleting.

You might even be unaware that you're in this situation. That is until the universe orchestrates some event to wake you up. Until you wake up, it's like being a prisoner in your own body. Some of you may not be unaware that your authentic self lies trapped beneath a façade—an alternative reality and identity that we create based on our protective ego instead of the deeper part of ourselves. Being comfortable, willfully unaware, and staying on the surface prevents us from getting to know ourselves. It feels easy to stay here, but is it? Sure, awakening takes work and requires lingering in uncertainty, but is that more work than sustaining a false sense of self?

It takes courage to build a deeper connection with yourself, to excavate and discover who you are. It takes small but mighty acts of courage every single day to be *You*, speak your truth instead of someone else's, and honor and leverage your natural gifts. This is not permission to say or do whatever you want without thought or consideration of how it affects others. In fact, growing self-awareness automatically contributes to empathy for others. Getting to know ourselves after a life of ignoring our genuine core is a process of unlearning, experimenting, digging deeper, contemplating one's current state, and thinking about doing things a little differently.

Small but mighty thoughts, acts, and experiences will help us create habits that allow us to show up more genuinely and in alignment with our sense of purpose. Remember we are living as a *part of* the universe and not merely *in* it. You are *that* important. Your ripple effect on those around you is based on how you show up. When we are our authentic selves and allow our superpowers to shine, we are less resistant, more receptive, and the thought of trying new things no longer threatens or tires us. We see change and uncertainty as opportunities for limitless possibilities. The result is a life with less fear, an enhanced ability to embrace this unfinished life, and fewer orange barrels and single lanes. Showing up authentically increases fulfillment, confidence, and the belief that we are enough. We embrace our gifts and know that others need them. We are no longer afraid of what we don't have. Instead, what we have and who we are exhilarate us.

Jumping off the cliff seems like a suitable metaphor for what it feels like in those moments full of life-changing potential. Do we say what we really think and take that leap, or do we stop at the edge because of our fears, which might include what others think about our choice or performance? Those moments should feel risky. Otherwise, they're not potentially life-changing. Do we take the risk by putting ourselves out there between the edge of the cliff and the surface of the water, not knowing the outcome? Are we willing participants in the new and ambiguous with intense anticipation of the consequences of our words or actions? My sister is her authentic self. She doesn't hold back, is a self-proclaimed over-sharer, and talks about whatever is going on in her head. It can wear thin sometimes (no offense, Sis) and be uncomfortable as she shares things about her life that I consider private or don't want to hear. Sometimes I want to put my hands over my ears and sing loudly, "La la la la la la la." I promise you, I am not saying anything here that would surprise her. She describes herself as weird. I tell her, "You are *You*." She has a solid sense of self. She displays her own intellect, creativity, and natural abilities. So do you. If we all lived as we truly are, no one would be weird because everyone would be weird.

She is courageous and committed to being her true self. Over my lifetime, this sister and I have had our challenges, but the more I make our relationship less about me and more about allowing her to be who she is, the stronger our relationship is. Sometimes she leaves three-minute messages on my voicemail because she needs to talk or process something out loud. She doesn't even care if I listen. Most times, I listen and feel it's a way I can honor who she is as her true self. Writing about this helps me process my role in being the best sister I can be for her on her journey, which has included lots of anxiety about the uncertainty of her new purpose. Her patience, trust in her inner being, and strong relationship with her *Self* opens possibilities. Her fire and clarity about her purpose and developing version of herself are showing up in powerful ways. She has a lot to offer the world. All of us do, and the best way to contribute our gifts is to recognize them, embrace them, and let them lead.

When you need a lift in spirit and a reminder that every moment matters, I offer you some reflections.

Summary

- *Don't overlook your daily small but mighty moments.* Acknowledge, honor, and celebrate them. Without them, achievement is not possible.
- *Small but mighty also applies to courage.* When life feels hard, do something brave, even if it's small. Courage strengthens our sense of self and helps us show up more authentically.
- *Small but mighty steps lead to a life of less resistance and fear,* more presence and fulfillment, and ultimately, more confidence and belief that we are enough as we are.
- *Don't allow the real You to be trapped beneath a façade.* Building your small but mighty muscle makes it easier to deal with uncertainty, see the possibilities, and close the gaps on your sense-of-self continuum.

PART FOUR
Be Messy. Be You.

CHAPTER ELEVEN

Give up on Perfect

> "Finding yourself" is not really how it works. You aren't a ten-dollar bill in last winter's coat pocket. You are also not lost. Your true self is right there, buried under cultural conditioning, other people's opinions, and inaccurate conclusions you drew as a kid that became your beliefs about who you are. "Finding yourself" is actually returning to yourself. An unlearning, an excavation, a remembering who you were before the world got its hand on you.
>
> —Emily McDowell

Practice does not make perfect. Forget about being perfect. Perfection means you're done. Done means nothing more, nothing better, status quo, and more of the same. Focus on progress—small but mighty steps in the right direction. I am a different person than I was five years ago. You are a different person than you were five years ago. My sense of self is stronger, and because of that, I show up differently from the inside out. On my journey to now, I have included more moments than I can count of reflection, self-talk, discovery, and tapping into myself and the amazing people who are my genuine cheerleaders.

I have devoted thousands of moments to building a deeper relationship with my *Self*, removed a lot of orange barrels, and widened many lanes on my way to possibilities-thinking. Also, I shifted expectations and increased my capacity to appreciate the now. My self-doubt continues to wane and my trust in my Self gets stronger every day, especially during times of uncertainty. Just knowing this makes me want to celebrate. Thinking about all the incremental moments that it took me to arrive at the present is dizzying. Small but mighty actions and bursts of courage have resulted in small but mighty progress that we cannot always see immediately. It doesn't matter how significant, visible, or tangible. Any time you are connecting with and learning about yourself, know it is significant.

Decluttering the Mind with a Shift in Thinking

As I tried to check in the night before a flight, I realized the name on my reservation did not match my legal ID. When the airline app on my phone didn't recognize my confirmation number, I began sweating. My mind went to many places, including an imagined scene where they wouldn't let me on the plane. I sweated even more when I expected not to make it to the client meeting the next morning. Then I recalled the saying that worrying is like praying for what you don't want. Being aware of my thoughts and feelings was progress and led to taking a deep breath and making a deliberate mindset shift. I could do nothing to change the situation, so I made sure I got to the airport a little early the next day. Of course, everything turned out fine, but without the mindset shift, I wouldn't have slept soundly that night.

Unhelpful thoughts and feelings create mind clutter that hinders us. How many times have you struggled to fall asleep because you couldn't put your mind to rest? Sleep is important to our well-being, and without it, we cannot show up fully. Catching myself in that moment and stopping the harmful mind-chatter was a small but mighty action that led to small but mighty progress in managing my personal stress. This is an example of one moment in which I chose how I showed up. For me, that was one pivotal, tiny moment that led to an enjoyable evening free of worry and with a good night's sleep. Isn't that worth recognizing and celebrating?

Resisting *YOU* Ultimately Leads to Dissatisfaction

One theme in this book is that building a stronger connection with yourself is good for all of us collectively. When we don't see and appreciate the good in ourselves, we sometimes pursue things that may, on the surface, make us feel good but undermine our deeper sense of self. We might make choices and desire things we think will make us happier, but because they meet only surface-level needs, our satisfaction is short-lived, and then we want more. What might you be sacrificing when your choices are not in alignment with your deeper *Self*?

Films are a substantial source of enjoyment for me, but I have noticed how they often mirror what's happening within and around the collective *us* at a deeper level. This makes sense since humans make movies. My daughter and I saw the latest Wonder Woman movie when it came out, despite the awful reviews.[37] *WW84* takes place in 1984, which becomes immediately obvious. My coming-of-age period was the 1980s. Who could mistake those hairstyles, shoulder pads, and music for any other decade?

This film brought to life a concept from Margaret Wheatley's book, *Who Do We Choose to Be?* Her reference to the "collapse of society" resonated with me in this superhero film.[38] In *WW84*, even Wonder Woman loses herself because of a preoccupation with something unattainable. She yearns to be with her soulmate, with whom she discovered love and developed a deep connection moments before he died.

Max, a key character and villain in the movie, receives a wish in which he can grant wishes for others. Unfortunately, Max's intentions are selfish because he does not grant wishes out of the goodness of his heart or to help others but for what he can get in return. Max focuses on the superficial, believing strength, wealth, power, and influence will define his success. Sadly, others bullied Max and called him a loser throughout his life. He had been living with a tremendous gap in his sense of self. Thus, he chooses money and power to make others value him. He wants to be a better father but mistakenly believes his young son will look up to him based on these possessions and the material things he will give him. Max doesn't realize his son wants plain old love and attention the most. We all can get caught up in false beliefs when we don't recognize our own pain and resist building a stronger connection with ourselves.

In the movie, Kristen Wiig plays Barbara, a clumsy, socially awkward, kind-hearted, and sweet person, who feels invisible in the presence of others. Barbara internalizes others' cruelty as statements of her unworthiness. She feels small when she's around others, and she cannot see her inner beauty, intelligence, and delightfulness, which shine as unique gifts. She becomes obsessed with being someone else: Wonder Woman. As you can guess, it doesn't work out so well.

For Wonder Woman, Max, and Barbara, seeking a sense of identity outside of their genuine selves has a cost, such as becoming intensely distracted with the unattainable, idealizing someone they perceive as superior, or accumulating only superficial things. The more powerful Max gets, the more his relationship with his son deteriorates. Wonder Woman's powers languish, and darkness, anger, and misery replace Barbara's passion, happiness, and love of life. The further they get from their true selves, the more disastrous their collective effect on their surroundings. They must turn inward.

WW84 seems to be a fitting metaphor for our society today. None of our lives are perfect, and we long for something different to escape the present and ourselves, which does more personal and societal harm than good. Appreciation for the small but mighty moments will strengthen the *Self* as you meander on the journey to your next best. Wonder Woman, Max, and Barbara eventually discover this truth. Of course, it's just a movie, but often the agenda of films is to reveal and make visible what is difficult for us to see.

What is truly important to you? Are you sure? Why? When you strive for what is inconsistent with your authentic inner being, you are sacrificing your own fulfillment and suppressing your individual and innate talents. Orange barrels pop up, and they block possibilities.

Normal Only Means Usual

Unexpected and unpleasant experiences or suffering can plague and clutter our minds with hopelessness, fatigue, and worry. Add to that the collective stress our world has endured (e.g., the pandemic), and we may increasingly wish time or our situation away, hoping for a better and more normal future state. We say things like, "I can't wait until this is over" or "When will things be back to normal?" What was once normal may never be again, and normal is also limiting. The expectation of normal, which only means usual, is an expectation that impedes possibilities. It is a façade based on the past. The past is done. If we base our sense of fulfillment on the past, we are not exercising possibilities-thinking, and we limit what could be our next best individual or collective thing.

Rather than depending on the past for what should be in the present and future, how about enjoying what *could* be? If we are only expecting the future to reflect the past, there is no room for exploration, experimentation, or better. Besides, the past doesn't exist except in our minds and in how we think about it. Every day presents an opportunity to try something different, make a choice about how we show up, reflect on our goodness and gifts, and exercise small but mighty actions and bursts of courage. Life is short, so act sooner than later.

You have choices, and as Eckhart Tolle in his book *The Power of Now* references, you can choose to resist or receive, accept and embrace, or change things.[39] Resistance narrows the road, making the journey more challenging and extending the time before you can live your fullest life. When we knock down the walls of resistance, we make room for clarity. Everyone experiences hardship, some more than others, and resisting makes it even harder. No matter what we do, it's there. When we cannot change the situation or our place in it, we can change how we might think about it.

Sometimes we can change the situation, but to gain clarity from the deeper part of ourselves, we must stop resisting the situation itself. I'm a different person than I was a few years ago. I am more me, more grateful and receptive, and I embrace more of life around me. And I'm more in the moment. I'm not perfect and still get stressed, worry, and sometimes resist life, but I am still exploring and experimenting. Often, I must remind myself to take a breath, do a stretch, and take care of myself. While I see possibilities, I have fewer expectations of how I think things should be and don't aim for normal or the way things always have been. My life feels nicer, easier, fuller, and amazing. This is not by accident; I got here by embracing the unfinished and learning to enjoy the journey a little more, bit by bit, and by growing and stretching my mind and perspective.

Try This

How are you doing at this point in the book? Use the space below to recognize and appreciate your unfinished life, the small but mighty actions you take, and the moments of courage you exercise. Appreciate all the moments in the space between the incremental steps on your journey in realizing and bringing to life your genuine *Self*.

- What steps have you taken since you began reading this book? What are you planning to do when you get to the end?

- What small experiments have you tried or will you try?

- How have you been courageous?

- What have you discovered about yourself, your uniqueness, and your talents? What do you know about your deeper self now that you didn't before?

- How were you showing up or positioning yourself at any time and especially in key moments? Has that changed? What will you try?

  _____
  _____
  _____

- What is an example of how you are shifting your expectations?

  _____
  _____
  _____

Take a moment now to recognize, appreciate, and celebrate your actions, discoveries, mindset shifts, and progress, no matter how small. Do a little dance, or have a glass of wine or a fancy coffee. Put it out there and make it known by writing it in a journal, telling someone, or saying it aloud.

Once again, reflect on your sense of self—how well you know yourself—in this moment and place an X on the continuum based on how clear, confident, and conscious you are about your *Self*, your genuine *Self*.

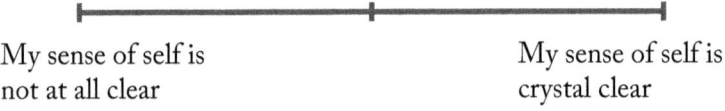

My sense of self is not at all clear   My sense of self is crystal clear

Is your X trending to the right? Is your gap narrowing? Maybe you took a little step back but don't fret; that's probably because you're more aware now. Hopefully, your placement of the X is trending toward the right, and over time you are sustaining a narrower gap. If not, revisit earlier chapters or other books or resources that better speak to you. Although there is no time like the present, this may not be the right time for you.

That's okay. You are on your own timeline and your own journey. Maybe there's just one thing you're ready to try, or you can put an item on your calendar to prompt you at some future date.

Remember, we are all works in progress. We're unfinished, and our sense of self will fluctuate based on situations, circumstances, and those who are around us by choice or not. Any movement to the right is progress and don't be worried about a periodic shift to the left. You are human. You've got this whether you've already started or will wait until you get to the end of the book. It's incremental. Just believe and trust in yourself and the process and remember the following points.

Summary

- *Forget about being perfect.* Perfection means you're done. Done means nothing more, nothing better, status quo, and more of the same. Focus on progress.
- *Shoot for recognizing small* and seemingly insignificant progress. It's mightier than you think. It doesn't matter how significant, visible, or tangible. Progress is progress, and it leads to the next thing.
- *None of our lives are perfect,* and longing for something different to escape the present and our *Self* does more personal and societal harm than good. Pretend you're sitting across the table from you. Have some empathy and give yourself a little pep talk.
- Don't fool yourself. *Sacrificing You has a significant effect* on your life and those you touch along the way. Don't give up.
- *There is so much more!* Seriously. What is normal but a façade based on the past? Are you really striving for the same? Your choices will either multiply the orange barrels and narrow the lanes or minimize and remove them. *Choose the authentic You.*

CHAPTER TWELVE

Be Unfinished

What lies behind us and what lies before us is tiny compared to what lies within you.

—*The Grizzlies* movie

This may be the last chapter, but metaphorically, this book remains unfinished, like our lives. We have more to talk about, be curious about, learn, observe, try, discover, and explore. So many more moments are ahead, so much more of me has yet to find its way to the surface, and so much more of you seeks to express itself. When I am no longer here on this Earth, I can be done, but not now. Not soon. I hope you are feeling the same. There is a reason we say "rest in peace" when people die.

Earlier in my career, I did a lot of international travel. My one trip to Peru was what inspired me to write this book. I never met my grandfathers while growing up because they died or left their families when my parents were young. When I met the general manager of our operations in Peru,

I instantly thought of him as someone who had the qualities and characteristics that I imagined a grandfather would have. In the day or so I spent in Peru, this man's ripple had a powerful effect on me. He made time for me and treated me as if I were family. Based on my experiences in previous companies, this was not common practice from someone at his level, especially not for someone in my role. He invited me to a local coffee shop to get to know me. While we were enjoying a treat and talking, he mentioned every person should do three things in their lifetime. The only one I remember was writing a book. His reasoning was that everyone has a story to tell that is theirs alone. I pinned this conversation on the bulletin board of my mind for at least fifteen years. Writing this book is yet another experiment in building a deeper relationship with my *Self*, learning about what is important to me, and showing up in life as my genuine self.

It's not an accident that I have arrived at my current state, one in which I would place the X further than ever before to the right on the sense-of-self continuum. Although this may change frequently based on my thoughts, feelings, and self-talk, the fluctuations happen less often, and I successfully continue to find a more permanent home on the right half of the continuum. Orange barrels and single lanes still show up, but I am more aware of them than ever, and through experimentation and trying many of the activities shared throughout this book, I remove or reduce them quickly and with increasing ease. Although it still shows its ugly head, perfection is becoming less of an expectation of myself, keeping frustration, depletion, and worry at bay. Shifting expectations, receiving what comes my way, and being present have required thousands of tiny moments of practice, self-awareness, and celebration.

Unhelpful thoughts, feelings, and experiences still find their way into my days. After all, I'm human, and I know ignoring them is an unrealistic expectation because they are there, regardless of whether I want them. Sweeping the undesired under the rug only provides temporary relief and may eventually become detrimental. Navigating through unpleasant emotions and self-doubt is how we continue to grow and connect with ourselves.

As I was working at the dining room table one afternoon and feeling overwhelmed by my day job, it just took one moment to feel at ease when a little bird appeared at the bottom of the patio door. It seemed to peek into my living room, maybe even at me. Then it flapped its wings and elevated itself to the level of the top of the dining table, continuing to peer into my space. The bird repeatedly alternated its position, lowering itself and hanging out at the bottom of the door and then flapping its wings to a higher position. You could experience this as a bird simply being a bird looking at its reflection in the glass. That sounds reasonable, and maybe that was exactly what happened, but I'll tell you what I believe.

This little bird appeared exactly when I needed a break from my anxiety. I needed a moment to breathe and refresh, and this was an opportunity to regroup and reground myself. The bird hung out there for a few minutes, and that was not an accident. The universe stepped in, and during that short time, I did nothing but watch the bird as it flapped its wings, moved up and down, and peered in the window or looked at the reflections in the glass (whatever your preference). I admired the bright yellow colors on its wings and quickly found my phone to take a couple of pictures. Besides feeling uplifted in that moment, the bird brought me and others joy over the next few days as I shared the pictures with my sisters and family.

A few days later, I told the story and showed the pictures to my sister-in-law while visiting with her. She brought out her book on Minnesota birds, and we spent twenty minutes identifying the bird and looking at others, which was pure enjoyment. That bird provided an escape from the moment, an opportunity to be present, and to receive and appreciate the moment—something I may not have done years earlier. Following that unexpected-bird moment, my mind was clear, my being was light, and my face was smiling. This was also an opportunity to carry over some newly found energy and a refreshed perspective into the rest of my workday. This little warbler reminded me of the power of being fully present.

This is one example of an infinite number of moments in our unfinished life journey when we can pause and then decide how to think, feel, and show up. It may be more difficult for some of us than others given personal circumstances. But if Eckhart Tolle could overcome living out of his car and wanting to commit suicide early in his life to build a deeper connection with himself and become an inspiring author who has enlightened millions, I am confident in myself and in you too. Thinking about living your purpose may feel like a lot of pressure. It seems big, ambiguous, mysterious, and complicated to achieve. Getting to know yourself in an incremental and progressive manner feels more doable and is at the root of living your purpose. You are unfinished, and while your idea of yourself will continue to develop, don't let that stop you from realizing and using your natural and unique strengths and gifts. The world—the universe—needs you and your ripple.

How are you feeling about the concept of unfinished? Are you seeing the possibilities? How are you shifting your mindset and expectations? How have you become more aware and reflective? If you haven't yet recognized and practiced the *small but mighty*, leveraging the power of the AND, asking for what you want, removing the phrase "should have" from your vocabulary, asking the universe for help, believing in and trusting the process, and soaking up all those words of encouragement and compliments from others, that's okay. Maybe the timing hasn't been quite right, and you'll put this book on the shelf and pick it up in a few days, months, or years when you are *feeling it*. That's okay too. I have been there.

Now is the best time to unleash your superpowers and let your true *Self* shine. Make a choice and, if you can, make it now. I believe in you. Believe in your *Self*. Choose tiny, achievable steps, small but mighty moments, acts of courage, and a life of imperfection, messiness, and endless potential.

Write your own book, literally or metaphorically. You have your unfinished story to tell. With a life full of experiments, discoveries, experiences, and meaning to reflect upon, you have value to add and gifts and talents to share with others.

There's no time like now to be unfinished.

End Notes

1. Tolle, Eckhart. *The Power of Now: A Guide to Spiritual Enlightenment.* California: Namaste Publishing and New World Library, 2004.
2. "Science: Down to the Science: Talent x Investment = Strength." *Gallup.* Accessed September 24, 2022. https://www.gallup.com/cliftonstrengths/en/253790/science-of-cliftonstrengths.aspx.
3. Jim Asplund. "How Your Strengths Set You Apart." *Gallup* November 5, 2021. https://www.gallup.com/cliftonstrengths/en/356810/strengths-set-apart.aspx#:~:text=in%2033%20million.-,In%20fact%2C%20the%20combinations%20of%20talents%20are%20so%20unique%20that,how%20people%20express%20their%20strengths.
4. "Find the CliftonStrengths Assessment That's Right For You." *Gallup.* Accessed October 2, 2022. https://www.gallup.com/cliftonstrengths/en/253868/popular-cliftonstrengths-assessment-products.aspx.
5. "Outcomes: 'Is CliftonStrengths evidence-based?' What people are *really* asking." *Gallup,* Accessed November 19,

6. Crystal Raypole. "'Who Am I?' How to Find Your Sense of Self." *Healthline.* June 17, 2020. https://www.healthline.com/health/sense-of-self.
7. Carolyn Gregoire. "How Being an Oldest, Middle or Youngest Child Shapes Your Personality: How Birth Order Affects Your Personality." *HuffPost.* Last modified May 15, 2015. https://www.huffpost.com/entry/birth-order-personality_n_7206252.
8. Chrissy Sexton. "Loving-kindness meditation increases positive emotions and happiness." *Earth.com.* September 26, 2020. https://www.earth.com/news/loving-kindness-meditation-increases-positive-emotions-and-happiness/.
9. Chopra, Deepak. *The Seven Spiritual Laws of Success.* California: Amber-Allen Publishing and New World Library, 1994.
10. Ibid
11. Kasee Bailey. "5 Powerful Health Benefits of Journaling." *Intermountain Healthcare.* July 31, 2018. https://intermountainhealthcare.org/blogs/topics/live-well/2018/07/5-powerful-health-benefits-of-journaling/.
12. Maurer Ph.D., Robert. *One Small Step Can Change Your Life: The Kaizen Way.* New York: Workman Publishing, 2004.
13. Marc Effron. "A Simple Way to Map Out Your Career Ambitions." *Harvard Business Review.* November 30, 2018. https://hbr.org/2018/11/a-simple-way-to-map-out-your-career-ambitions.
14. Nabin Paudyal. "Here's Why Writing Down Your Goals Really Does Work." *Lifehack.* Last modified March 16, 2022. https://www.lifehack.org/385087/heres-why-writing-down-your-goals-really-does-work.
15. Crystal Raypole. "How Many Thoughts Do You Have Each Day? And Other Things to Think About." *Healthline.*

February 28, 2022. https://www.healthline.com/health/how-many-thoughts-per-day.
16 Wickman, Gino. *Traction: Get a Grip on Your Business.* Texas: BenBella Books, Inc., 2011.
17 Ibid
18 Chopra, Deepak. *The Seven Spiritual Laws of Success.* California: Amber-Allen Publishing and New World Library, 1994.
19 Tolle, Eckhart. *A New Earth: Awakening to You Life's Purpose.* London, England: Penguin Life, 2006.
20 "Renew Yourself - Body, Mind, And Spirit: Day 8 - Caring for the Mind." *Scribd.* Accessed November 4, 2022. Renew Yourself - Body, Mind, and Spirit | PDF | Self Esteem | Stress (Biology) (scribd.com).
21 "Multitasking: Switching costs – Subtle "switching" costs cut efficiency, raise risk. *American Psychological Association.* March 20, 2006. https://www.apa.org/topics/research/multitasking#:~:text=Thus%2C%20multitasking%20may%20seem%20efficient,percent%20of%20someone's%20productive%20time.
22 Silver, Tosha. *Outrageous Openness: Letting the Divine Take the Lead.* New York: Atria Paperback, 2015.
23 Ibid
24 Silver, Tosha. *It's Not Your Money: How to Live Fully from Divine Abundance.* New York: Hay House, 2019.
25 Wheatley, Margaret J. *Who Do We Choose To Be? Facing Reality, Claiming Leadership, Restoring Sanity.* California: Barrett-Koehler Publishers, Inc., 2017.
26 *Iron Man.* Directed by Jon Favreau. 2008. Burbank, CA: Marvel Studios.
27 *The Last Full Measure.* Directed by Todd Robinson. 2019. Los Angeles, CA: Roadside Attractions.
28 Wheatley, Margaret J. *Who Do We Choose To Be? Facing Reality, Claiming Leadership, Restoring Sanity.* California: Barrett-Koehler Publishers, Inc., 2017.

29. Chopra, Deepak. *The Seven Spiritual Laws of Success.* California: Amber-Allen Publishing and New World Library, 1994.
30. Tolle, Eckhart. *The Power of Now: A Guide to Spiritual Enlightenment.* California: Namaste Publishing and New World Library, 2004.
31. Chopra, Deepak. *The Seven Spiritual Laws of Success.* California: Amber-Allen Publishing and New World Library, 1994.
32. Ibid
33. Ibid
34. Ibid
35. Wheatley, Margaret J. *Who Do We Choose To Be? Facing Reality, Claiming Leadership, Restoring Sanity.* California: Barrett-Koehler Publishers, Inc., 2017.
36. Ibid
37. *Wonder Woman 1984.* Directed by Patty Jenkins. 2020. Burbank, CA: Warner Brothers.
38. Wheatley, Margaret J. *Who Do We Choose To Be? Facing Reality, Claiming Leadership, Restoring Sanity.* California: Barrett-Koehler Publishers, Inc., 2017.
39. Tolle, Eckhart. *The Power of Now: A Guide to Spiritual Enlightenment.* California: Namaste Publishing and New World Library, 2004.

www.ingramcontent.com/pod-product-compliance
Lightning Source LLC
LaVergne TN
LVHW012019060526
838201LV00061B/4374